BUDGET YOUR GOALS

NOT YOUR SILVER

H. DOYLE SMITH

BUDGET YOUR GOALS NOT YOUR SILVER
Copyright © 2024 **H. Doyle Smith**

ISBN (Paperback): 978-1-964494-16-6
ISBN (Hardback): 978-1-964494-15-9
ISBN (Ebook): 978-1-964494-17-3

Printed in the United States of America.

PROMINENT
BOOKS
EDGE

5830 E 2nd St, Ste 7000 #9983
Casper, WY 82609
USA

CONTENTS

Process Economics 1
Preface... 7
America—Love It and Improve It 11

PART ONE
Introduction

Chapter One: What's This Book About?....................... 19

PART TWO
Your Personal Economy

Chapter Two: Making Money Is Illegal 31
Chapter Three: Twelve Keys to Getting Anything Done.......... 40
Chapter Four: Have You Got What It takes?.................... 58
Chapter Five: The Mathematical Scissors...................... 76
Chapter Six: I'd Rather Be (You Name It) 90
Chapter Seven: Budget Your Goals, Not Your Silver............. 97

PART THREE
You and Everyone Else

Chapter Eight: Economic Structures 111
Chapter Nine: Demand... 129
Chapter Ten: Money 135

Chapter Eleven: Economies of Scale............................ 142
Chapter Twelve: On the Matter of Waste and Risk............... 148
Chapter Thirteen: The Inevitable Monopoly....................... 155
Chapter Fourteen: The Current Nature of Value 171
Chapter Fifteen: More About Money............................. 175
Chapter Sixteen: Zen versus the Apocalypse.................... 187
Chapter Seventeen: The Nature of Vestment........................ 196

PART FOUR
Investments We Need to Make as a Country

Chapter Eighteen: What Do We Need to Do? 201

Conclusion 219
From and About the Author 221

Dedicated to Dolores Jane Hill

PROCESS ECONOMICS

VALUE

THERE IS A stream flowing behind my house. The bed of that stream is covered with gravel. It's pretty to look at but serves no purpose otherwise.

I have a driveway in front of my house. After long use the gravel in that driveway has been pushed down in the ground so that in wet weather the driveway is very muddy and when it is dry the dust gets on things in the house.

I get a wheelbarrow and dig out the gravel in the creek bed. Now the gravel has a use, and I use that resource to accomplish the objective of restoring my driveway. This is an economic transaction.

How do I know this? The alternative is to use my relationship with my boss to work to acquire currency. I can then use that currency to pay someone to move that gravel for me. Those actions create data, and the data is reflective of an economic transaction.

If I use currency to describe this transaction the data involved appears twice, once when I earn the money and once when I pay for moving the gravel. If I use my wheelbarrow and time, it does not appear in any data.

Data economics, in which the transaction is the exchange of currency for goods and services, is reflective of the economy, and gives us an idea of what is going on in the economy. It does not work outside of data economics, and most economies do not use currency. When I first proposed that we look at value, rather than currency, my professor told me, "You have to stop somewhere." The study of "value" goes beyond the confines of data economics and requires an understanding of the nature of the objective. in the redefinition of economics. To deal with non-monetary economies requires going on when you would rather stop. The value of any resource is its ability to be used to accomplish an objective. It is important to understand the difference between "resources" and "goods and services."

When I hire a lobbyist to speak for me with a politician. The value of the lobbyist's relationship to the politician is a "resource." When he gets paid for using that "resource," it becomes a "service." The difference is significant. I can approach the politician myself, establish a relationship with him and use that relationship to establish contact with the politician, but the value o that relationship exists only when there is an objective for which it can be used.

In the case involving gravel above, I have used a resource to accomplish an objective, a sound gravel driveway. The use of a resource to accomplish an objective ends up being the definition of an economic transaction. The *value* of any *resource* lies in its ability to be *used* to *accomplish* an *objective*.

A BACKWATER OF WORLD WAR II

World War II was fought from Moscow, across Europe and the Atlantic, to the Pacific, Japan, China and even to India. In this vast expanse, some locations were left isolated. One such location was the island of Mindanao in the Philippines. John Keats wrote about this area in the book, THEY FOUGHT ALONE.

Wendel Fertig was a businessman, who was left behind when the Americans retreated from the country. After establishing radio contact with American forces, Fertig was given a commission as a Coronel. The book describes the fighting there, but one theme of the book dealt with the economic arrangement that made the Philippinos economically strong even while the Japanese held the upper hand militarily.

The basis for the success of this economic arrangement was the designation of the worth of the dollar as equal to a bushel of rice or a bushel of corn. There were four things about this designation that made the economy successful.

Value is the ability of a resource to accomplish an objective. The objective of both rice and corn was to eliminate hunger. We are hungry at least three times every day, Since the dollar was equivalent to a resource that had value at lest three times every day, it maintained its value over time.

Both rice and corn were available to everyone. These were a common crop on the Island, and everyone could acquire these crops easily. If a crop has no value and is not available it cannot be used as a basis for an economy.

The crop could not be accumulated. In 1930, the Smoot-Hawley tariff placed such a burden on foreigners that they could not sell their products in the United States. As a result, the medium of exchange was collected in Fort Knox as the foreign companies paid for their purchases in gold. The result was that there was no currency circulating outside that Fort. There was no currency available to pay for the transportation of food from Florida to New York, so the crops were rotting in the fields in Florida, while people were starving in New York.

Last, the value of the dollar was designated. That value of a dollar in Mindanao during World War II was designated as worth one bushel of either rice or corn.

Now, you will note that we have two resources, corn and rice involved. It was not the resource that gave value to the dollar, but the objective.

The economy that developed on Mindanao during World War II came to a crashing halt.

One soldier was offered the service of having his clothes washed and gave the woman soap. Soap was rare on Mindanao and the woman felt that she had been paid a lot for her service.

A second soldier, offered the same service, accepted but gave the woman nothing. A third soldier gave the woman who offered the same service $50.

So was the value of the dollar a bushel of rice, nothing, soap, or one fiftieth of a wash?

Without a set value to the dollar, the economy collapsed.

PETROLEUM AS THE RESOURCE FOR VALUATION

When we look at the American economy in history we fand that a similar mechanism made the United States economy strong for many years.

There are two elements here. One is currency, The other is valuation of the resources.

Currency is designated currency, but it cannot be valued by its ability to be used to accomplish an objective. Gold is a good currency, since it has

3

a designated value, but it is not used up by application of the rules of value. It is not used up. Currency is something that will be received by a person, stored until needed, and then used in a exchange for other resources. If the gold that backs the value of the currency is made into jewelry, it will not serve again as currency. It has a designed relationship to the dollar, but as objectives are found, its value goes up. If those objectives are accomplished and not continued, the value of the currency goes down.

The value of the dollar is a different matter. The book THEY FOUGHT ALONE illustrates that the value of a dollar, to be strong needs to be tied to a value of a continuing objective. In the case of Mindanao during World War II, that value was based on the continuing objective of eliminating hunger.

In the United States, after the Civil war, John D Rockefeller acquired a monopoly in oil. He set the price of that oil at twenty-eight dollars a barrel. Oil was used to heat homes and provide light at night. This was a continuing objective, so anyone could compare the value of other objectives and establish a value for it.

This understanding provided a continuing value for oil. It had value, that is it could be used to accomplish an objective and the objective was continuing. It was available; the Standard Oil Trust provided it was available to all at a standard price. It could not be accumulated. People had no normal way of storing oil. And it had a designated price.

This understanding of the valuation of the dollar is a useful mechanism for understanding any economy. The fact that there are two different mechanisms involved helps illustrate the problem of competing definitions.

In a currency economy, there must be currency to use for exchange. In 1930 Congress enacted the Smoot-Hawley tariff. The price of anything made in a foreign country was increased by the amount of the tariff to the point that no foreign production could be used to purchase products made in the United States. To make a purchase then, the foreign customer needed to use currency. Since there was only a limited amount of currency available, that currency was accumulated as purchases were made. The currency did not return to be used in commerce, and the Great Depression followed. There was no value in any one commodity so there was no way to allow commerce to continue.

The interaction between the use of currency and the valuation of the objective is one way of understanding the study recounted in the appendix.

The concern of the constituents about affordable housing and homelessness, while the representative did not include it in his concerns results from the constituents valuing the objective of having a safe and comfortable place to stay. That objective is in direct contradiction to the objective of the moneyed interest in maximizing the accumulation of currency.

Maximizing the accumulation of currency results in much money being accumulated in bank accounts where it is not accessible to use. In the same way as the accumulation of money caused the great depression by making that currency, the accumulation of funds in banks removes the amount of useable currency.

THE EFFECT OF TAXES

The tenant's objective in a rental situation is to find a warm and safe place to stay. This objective is recognized when we use process economics. The landlord's objective is to maximize his bank account. Right away we find that we are confronted with a conflict of interest.

A certain property in Cuyahoga County, Ohio consists of a five-story building rented to seniors. The landlord has allowed the elevator in this building to be out of service for a considerable time. The seniors who rent apartments on the fifth floor are required to use the stairs when they leave the building, effectively isolating those with problems walking up and down stairs.

Repairs to those elevators cost money and reduce the accumulation of currency for the landlord. At the same time resources available to the tenant are limited.so he cannot make those repairs himself. This conflict of interest between the objectives of the landlord and the objectives of the tenant allow the landlord to extort the maximum currency from the tenant while not providing the tenant with what he is paying for.

This situation is condoned by the Internal Revenue Service tax code. The landlord is considered a "passive" investor. If the services needed were provided by anyone other that the owner, the receipts would be taxed for employment or Social Security. Because he is the owner his receipts are not taxed. This means that he has a tax advantage of at least 13.5% of his income. The tax law encourages the landlord to ignore the repairs needed and pocket the difference.

CONCLUSION

The idea that data economics alone is the only way to look at our economy establishes a conflict of interest that divides our people into wealthy and poor. It needs to be studied, and appropriate changes made.

PREFACE

Things are frequently what they seem.
And this is fortune's frown.
While only the game fish swims upstream
The sensible fish swims down.
—Ogden Nash

IF YOUR ECONOMIC bathtub is dry, you've been taken to the cleaners, but you have not gotten clean. People think of their economic situation as if they got more money, they would be happier, and it's possible they would. But economic security is never based on the one-time acquisition of funds. Your economic situation can be compared to a bathtub. The bathtub has a faucet. That faucet puts water into the bathtub. It also has a drain that allows water to leave. If the drain is closed, water accumulates. So it is the same with your economic situation. If your outgo, the drain, exceeds your income, the faucet, your upkeep, becomes your downfall, but if your income exceeds your outgo, no matter how much the difference, you are economically sound.

The same applies to a marriage, a partnership, a corporation, or any other combination of people whose economic situation can be studied. Eventually, the overall economy of the world is a combination of these individual economies.

There is order in the world. Those who believe that the world works are right. The problem arises when people think more highly of themselves than they ought to think (a phrase from the biblical book of Romans 12:3, to be exact.) Such thinking leads people to see that the world is as they want it to be and not as it really is. Such thinking overlooks many clues about how the world works and supposes that even though we have only seen a small part of it and we understand less, we are able to insist that it abide by our rules.

There are two questions in philosophy that illustrate the difference in these points of view. One, "If a man does something and no woman is present, is he still wrong?" is clearly a joke. The other is, "If a tree falls in the woods and there is no one to hear it, is there still a sound?" René Descartes would say, "No, it is our hearing it that makes it a sound." John Locke would say, "No, it is our hearing it that makes it a sound."

In this book, we are discussing a subject that has a mechanism and exists outside our ability to understand. It would appear to require the first point of view. However, because we act on our understanding and it is our actions that matter, we need to use the second.

The author has been making observations over sixty years and has developed certain principles that tend to explain some of the results of his observations. These principles seem to work, but please use it as a reference of probabilities rather than an authority or rule of law. Since the message is more important than the messenger, further discussion of the author's qualifications must wait for an epilogue.

Those principles are not the principles of the academician. Academic studies from books are not comprehensive enough to cover all the possible combinations that exist in reality. Even a lifetime of study has not made everything apparent to the author, but the exposure of fifty years' experience has provided a far wider range of experience than a four-year exposure in college would provide. For this reason, these discussions, even though they have a relationship to other books, are far more influenced by actual observation.

If the principles that underlie this book are not understood, the conclusions will seem to be absurd to some and idiotic to others, so the first part of the book will deal with what are often called academic matters. Don't let that scare you. Descriptions of the importance of the economic structure, the process by which economic decisions are made, the mathematical scissors, the inevitable monopoly, and several other concepts are probably better understood by the individuals that they realize, even though the relationship of the income tax exemption for principle residence to homelessness will be a surprise. That this income tax exemption has been a major cause of homelessness will appear later.

This does not mean that such an exemption should be eliminated, but that other changes would make other businesses profitable once more.

There is a story of a leprechaun who was forced to reveal where he had hidden his gold. The Irishman marked the tree and made the leprechaun vow that he would not touch the mark or the tree. The leprechaun lived up to his vow, but made the same mark on every other tree. So it is with many conclusions of this book. Keep what is good, and make it better.

AMERICA— LOVE IT AND IMPROVE IT

ALTHOUGH THE BOOK is about how things work, it is also a book about flaws—flaws in the American economic system. These flaws encourage drug use, eliminate vital functions, make prison a great place to be, and allow things to get out of balance and out of hand. It takes an understanding of drugs to understand why no user will turn in as pusher. It takes just such an understanding to realize why a person is better off in prison than on his own resources. It is difficult to realize that every economic activity gravitates toward monopoly and, eventually, rebellion against monopoly. These things are the subject of this book.

These are flaws in the system. No one can dispute that. Any system that exists has flaws. To identify them, we need an understanding of how the system works. It is difficult for most people to understand how the whole economic system works because they are only exposed to small parts of it, and those parts limit them to knowledge of how their particular part works. Some of the best comments the author has heard about the system, however, come from factory workers who described the difficulties they endured during the Carter administration. It is possible for people to understand how the overall system works, especially where it applies to them if they are exposed to principles.

This book has no bibliography for a number of reasons. First, the book is a result of fifty years of actual experience, informed observations, and trained readings. In the legal profession, one basic legal principle is that the evidence used should be the "best evidence." Despite normal preference for "authoritative statement," I find that "authorities" have only learned what they have been exposed to, limited their comments to what they consider important, used language that can cover only part of the experience, and allowed the reader to interpret what he wrote in accordance to his own language, ability, and preferences. For these reasons, the best evidence appears to be the actual experience, followed by informed observations. Only when readings correspond to the better evidence should the reader give them authoritative status. We expect the reader, in this case, to use his intelligence to form his understanding.

Books with bibliographies refer to subjects that have been discussed before. The area that this book discusses, the dynamics of the period between economic transactions, is new. The ideas have been referred to as Keynesian, but John Maynard Keynes wrote at a time when it was necessary to raise people to a level above that threshold amount that would allow economic activity to exist. The conditions that existed then do not exist now. To approach this book with the idea that others have written about the subject before is to fail to begin to understand what is written in it.

During the last forty years, many concepts that are used here have been the result of reading other authors' books. At times, the best way to describe an idea is the way some other author wrote, and the same words have been chosen to incorporate the idea in this book. As a result, some ideas may sound like plagiarism. If another author wants credit for a specific area, it will be given…if he can show me the source he claims is used here. Be assured, however, that no book was in front of the author when he wrote. He has deliberately used other books only where passages were scanned into a computer (and credit given). No matter how important a book is to this subject, there is no way to remember the reference if the book was read many years ago. A bibliography that fails to give accurate information as to its source cannot be considered reliable.

Another reason for the omission of a bibliography is that there are no comparable books. Typically, economics has been considered under either macroeconomics or microeconomics. Macroeconomics deals with the overall economic activity of an economic unit. Microeconomics deals with the best way for a company to remain solvent. Both are valid and vital subjects to review and study, as well as basic subjects for the survival of an economy. However, both assume demand, and both rely on the law of large numbers to give statistical probabilities of what is happening. This book is based on the understanding of the individual basis of demand and the mechanics of its development. Statistics and mathematics do not apply to the logical activities of the individual mind. This book is related to conventional economics as an atom is related to an automobile.

Because of the size of the book, there are probably repetitions. Sometimes the same words can describe two or more concepts. At other times, repetition makes the book more readable. And repeating a phrase just because it sounds good is possible. The subject of this study is very important, but the smoothness in style is not nearly as important as the common sense that is placed in the content. Moreover, the author likes to put something in his books for everyone, and some people enjoy looking for faults.

Because the author has been exposed to so many different influences in writing this book, it is hard to recognize every person who has made it possible. Sixty years is a long time, and many of the influences have been significant without even being noticed at the time they happened. The author has a memory of a sixth grade teacher who insisted he had the ability to learn easily. Twenty-five years later, he remembered the conversation that made such a difference, and Mrs. Roberts's influence is noted.

There are also individuals whose influence has been totally negative, but without their influence, things that taught concepts could not have happened. Since one should be silent about anyone if there is nothing good you can say about them, they will receive mental thanks, but will not be exposed to censure.

It is important to remember some of those whose contributions have made the book possible. Without the support and encouragement of the author's wife, Dolores Hill, there would have been no possibility of recording the results of fifty years of observation, study, and organization.

PART ONE

INTRODUCTION

The Blind Men and the Elephant

John Godfrey Saxe

It was six men of Hindostan,
To learning much inclined,
Who went to see the elephant,
(Through all of them were blind);
That each by observation
Might satisfy his mind.
The first approached the elephant,
And happening to fall
Against his broad and sturdy side,
At once began to bawl,
"Bless me, it seems the elephant
Is very like a wall"
The second, feeling of his tusk,
Cried, "Ho! What have we here
So very round and smooth and sharp?
To me 'tis mighty clear
This wonder of an elephant
Is very like a spear."
The third approached the animal,
And happening to take
The squirming trunk within his hands,
Then boldly up and spake;
"I see," quoth he, "The elephant
Is very like a snake."
The fourth stretched out his eager hand
And felt about the knee,
"What most this mighty beast is like
Is mighty plain," quoth he;
"Tis clear enough the elephant
Is very like a tree."
The fifth, who chanced to touch the ear
Said, "Even the blindest man
Can tell what this resembles most;
Deny the fact who can,

This marvel of an elephant
Is very like a fan."
The sixth no sooner had begun
About the beast to grope
Then, seizing and the swinging tail
That fell within his scope,
"I see," cried he, "the elephant
Is very like a rope.
And so these men of Hindostan
Disputed loud and long,
Each of his own opinion
Exceeding stiff and strong,
Though each was partly in the right,
And all were in the wrong!

CHAPTER ONE

What's This Book About?

St. Peter's Church in Canton, Ohio, was a beautiful building. One day, without warning, a part of the steeple fell on the sidewalk. After studying the structure, architects found that the individual bricks were not made to last and had given way because they had been unable to sustain themselves or provide support for the others around them. The church building was made of these bricks, and the "survival" of the whole depended on the "health" of each brick.

In the same way, the survival of an economy is dependent on the economic health of the individual in the economy. When people can contribute to a society, they become a drain on it by, for example, their being unable to provide more to the economy than they need to survive in it. That is, their outgo is greater than their income. If their income is so small that all they can do is survive, they can contribute to their society by not claiming things that others must supply. Their inability to contribute makes society less able to improve itself. Truly, every individual is important to an economy, just as each break was important to the survival of St. Peter's Church. You are an individual in your economy and important to it!

To understand the reality of how each of us is important to our economy, we need to study economics. Economics, which is sometimes called the dismal science, has many definitions. To most people, it is the study of how exchanges happen in any of a number of ways, each requiring a certain set of definitions, each definition related to those exchanges. So I give money to you for something of value to me. You give up that money for something to you. As this process continues, each transaction moves through the cycle until some of that money returns to you. Macroeconomics, the study of how the whole monetary system works, and microeconomics, the study of how an individual business operates within the monetary system, are dependent on the exchange. Each system assumes that demand and supply is there.

This book deals with economics in a different way. In each exchange mentioned above, there are at least two participants, and there is a period of time between transactions for each participant. The transaction period for each starts with a person giving up something of value (a resource) for money, and the period ends with giving up money to acquire something that will help them accomplish an objective.

We are not dealing with the exchange, but a period between changes. For that reason, definitions based on the old system of exchange do not work. For example, if money is defined as a medium of exchange and there is no exchange, money would appear to be irrelevant. A new definition is required, which is "money is a reference point or benchmark for value." This shows the reason that money can be a medium of exchange. People can refer to their money and use the understood value of that money to compare what they want to what they are willing to give up. When money meets the criteria to be a reference point of value, it becomes a medium of exchange. Until it meets that criterion, it is only one of many commodities whose value changes from day to day. Any person can relate everything else to a benchmark and assign a value relative to that benchmark to every other need that they have. Secondarily, since the same benchmark is used by others, elements of exchanges are related to similar benchmarks and provide a common understanding between participants. During the time between exchanges, money is used to determine relative value and, as a result, demand.

Most economists are mathematicians. They try to determine how much of an item can be made and sold at a profit, or how much incentive is needed to keep the economy running strong. To do this, they need to assume that a demand for products exist and try to determine the amount of that demand. This book, on the other hand, looks at what causes an individual transaction to occur and the mechanics that happen when a transaction is being considered; that is, the period between exchanges and the way demand develops. Because of this difference, mathematics is inappropriate. Logic, along with psychology, becomes much more important and relevant.

What does cause a transaction to occur, and what are the mechanics behind it?

YOUR FINANCES IN A NEW LIGHT

Exchanges are transactions, but what is a transaction? This question alone gives us food for thought. To pay someone to mow the lawn is a transaction. One definition of the word could be to give up something for something else. Before the transaction, the buyer had an unkempt lawn and money. The seller didn't have the money before the swap, but had it after. The buyer, however, could have had the same result by mowing the yard himself. From the buyer's point of view, the transaction involved the exchange of a resource, either time or money for a mowed lawn. Whether anyone else is involved is immaterial. So we need a new definition of a transaction. Here's the one possibility.

Uncle Hascue and Aunt Flora lived on a thirteen-acre farm in North Carolina. They saved seeds from one year to the next, had a cow, raised a few pigs, and generally had no need for money. They were quick to complain about the amount of income that qualified as poverty level, established by the government since their own life did not require very much. Flora said that they had never had $600 in any one year. Because they didn't travel, buy groceries, go to movies, or have any other significant reasons to spend money, they managed well on the little money they had. By keeping their truck and maintaining it themselves, caring for their tools, and sewing their own clothes, they eliminated even more expenses. Their resources included the land itself, their knowledge of what that land could produce, and their willingness to eliminate expenditure that other people consider necessary. They had many resources but little money.

Uncle Hascue and Aunt Flora lived well on their thirteen acres. Their resources included a clear title to the land, knowledge of what vegetables would thrive in the soil on their farm, how to care for breed livestock, knowledge of how to preserve the land, a "lifestyle" discipline that eliminated unnecessary spending, friendship with those who might have reason to cause them harm, and many other specifics that worked in their favor. All these things were vested in their estate, but would never have been written down or known to those who were not involved in their lives. To this was added their time, their patience, and their confidence in themselves. Sometimes they used their time to help others and were paid without reporting the payment, and sometimes the produce that they raised (especially tobacco) was exchanged for money. This money in turn was exchanged for other things they could not raise themselves. Their life was spent on the edge of the money economy and, like most people's lives, was imperfectly connected to it.

For Uncle Hascue and Aunt Flora, all their resources were enough to cover all their needs. So it is with all of us, unless we are impoverished.

We have heard that another definition of economics is the study of the distribution of scarce resources, and that is true: scarcity has become a major element of pricing, which comes from demand. However, demand creates scarcity, while scarcity, surprisingly, does not create demand. To illustrate this, we need to heat the story of the five farmers.

Al, Ben, Charley, Dan, and Ed had gone to high school together and had farmed in the same area for fifty years. All of them decided to retire, and each had to determine what to do with his farm. Al had a son, Frank, who had worked with him on the farm and was willing to care for him from his retirement on. So Al deeded the farm to Frank. Frank's resource for acquiring the farm was his relationship with his father.

Ben heard that George, an agriculture student at Iowa State, wanted to buy a farm. Ben contacted him and gave him the farm with the assurance that George would pay him so much each month for the rest of his life. Since Ben knew that George was a good farmer, Ben was willing to take the chance. George's resource for acquiring the farm was his knowledge of farming.

Charlie contacted Harry, who owned a retirement home. He made an agreement to exchange the farm for lifetime care at the home. Harry's resource was his ability to provide long-term care.

Dan and Ed offered their farms on the open market. Ed knew he would need to have $400,000 to take care of himself for life, while Dan already had savings and felt he could survive on $200,000. Ian was interested in a farm and offered each of them $300,000. Dan accepted, and Ed declined.

At this point, we note that there has been a demand for each farm except for Ed's. There is no scarcity of farms, yet there has been demand for them, so scarcity can hardly be the reason for demand.

Soon after this, however, Jake and Larry decide to go farming. Ed's farm was the only farm available. Jake had about $500,000 in the bank, but did not want to spend all of it, so he offered Ed $450,000. Larry had only $100,000, but he was willing to borrow so he could offer the same amount. After contacting both men to tell them he had equal offers, Larry increased his bid. Ed accepted Larry's increased offer. Even though scarcity didn't affect demand, it did affect price.

The sale brings up another important part of the equation: value. Value is a range between the highest acceptable price of the buyer and the lowest acceptable price of the seller, while price is the fixed amount of the transaction when it is completed. Price and value are not the same.

Most people understand the ideas behind these differences, but may resist accepting the concepts in this book because they're invested heavily in the current understanding. Most people see the difference between value and price, but because value is not clear (and cannot be clear because the definition of value keeps changing depending on the thing itself and what the buyers and sellers put on it) they use price to approximate value. The result, in some cases, is a desire to know what a seller paid for what he is selling and an attempt to relate the buyer's value to the seller's cost. This is done by both the buyer and seller. Value is related to price at the moment of a transaction, yet the value range includes such a large number of possibilities that even a moment later, the value has changed so much that there is no relationship between them. (I'll talk more about value later in the book.)

And so we can look at the nature of demand, logically rather than mathematically, by how five men deeded or sold their farms through methods that did not conform to the laws of macroeconomics and microeconomics. In those cases, the subject is ordinarily based upon the transaction at the point where supply and demand meet. This book is about the economic structure, where demand is developed and supply determined.

Among the points covered by this book, you will find these ideas—some of them controversial—briefly summed up here and expanded upon in later chapters:

- Money is not first a medium of exchange, but first a reference point for determination of value; that is, specific demand for an item. This determination is made both by the buyer and seller separately. Money allowing people to refer to the same point when discussing the possibility of an exchange becomes a medium of exchange.

- Monopoly is not only inevitable, but is the only logical result of stable economic activity.
- Price and value are completely separate, different in character, and appear at different times.
- Scarcity has little reason to cause or limit a transaction unless specific objectives cause the scarcity. The specific objectives are the essence of demand. Once decided on, these objectives may cause scarcity.
- The minimum wage is both the backing for the dollar in the United States and the cause of depopulation of the countryside.
- Social Security and welfare in the United States, as are other conditions that equate to these in post-Armada Spain, are both the mainstay of American financial stability and the cause of domestic business failures.
- The inevitable cycle of anarchy, stability, monopoly, and return to anarchy is the prevalent mechanism that controls human history.

This is not a standard interpretation of economics, and I understand how you may try to reconcile it with the economics you are familiar with. I share some of the basic ideas with the standard interpretations and ask that you suspend preconceived ideas and conclusions to get the most from my studies.

One shift in focus from conventional economics to demand economics is to change from understanding the nature of a transaction to an understanding of the participants in a transaction. I know this shift is a drastic one. First, participants in a transactions are so different and so varied in the way they arrive at the decision to enter a transaction that the analysis may seem to be overwhelming. It would be easy to give up and just assume that demand exists, rather than to continue to look for the elements that are needed for economic activity. Surprisingly, a framework of concepts does exist.

WHEN PEOPLE CAN'T

Economics requires more resources for each individual than he needs to survive. Without those resources, people rebel against their conditions. History has a lot to say about "when people can't."

The fall of the Roman Empire has usually been ascribed to military might of the Franks, but the writings of Ammianus Marcellinus, a Roman historian, describe a time when the emperor Julian was forced to put down a mutiny of his soldiers caused by the failure of grain to arrive from Aquitaine. The mutiny was stopped only when a shipment arrived. This reinforces the idea that it is the economic activity that shapes history and not the military.

Moses Hadas, in his historical study A History of Rome, quoted a Latin panegyric from the time of the Emperor Constantine:

> Another panegyrist, speaking before Constantine at Autun in A.D. 311, mentions the desolation the Bagaudae had wrought in Bourgogne:
>
> Land which has never repaid cultivation is necessarily abandoned, and so it is when impoverished farmers are so weighed down by debt that they are not free to channel water or clear brush; and so soil that was once tolerable is sunk in marshes or overrun with brambles. But even the famous region (of Beaune and Chalon-sur-Saone) is smitten with sterility. Its lowest portion has some vines, but to the rear all the rest is forest and inaccessible rocks, the haunts of wild beasts. The plain at the foot of the hills stretching to the Saone was at one time, I hear, a flourishing place. Constant care in each farm kept the channels clear to drain the flow of the springs. Now it is abandoned and the channels are choked: the rich bottom land has been turned into a swamp.
>
> Even the vines which the ignorant admire so are grown too old respond to cultivation...Why should I speak of other localities on that area? You have confessed that they brought tears to your eyes. You saw no cultivated, cleared, flourishing land, no easy roads, no navigable rivers washing the very gates of towns, but immediately after the fork of the road to Belgium everything was desolate, uncared for, rank, mute, and dismal. Even the military roads were so rough and hilly and broken as not to admit half-loaded or even empty carts.

This was a situation where farmers could not provide for the recultivation of their fields and necessarily indicated that production on these farms slowly decreased. Because of the failure to maintain the relationship between revenues and expenses for those farmers who were required to do the work, Gaul fell. The idea that the withdrawal of support by those who could no longer live under the Roman system was the cause of the fall of the Western Roman Empire rather than military activity is a valid possibility, at least in Gaul. This is further supported by Salvian, a later Roman writer (also quoted by Moses Hadas) who comments less than 150 years later:

> All the while the poor are despoiled, widows groan, orphans are trodden underfoot, to the degree that many—and these of good birth and liberal education—flee to the enemy to avoid death by official persecution. They seek among barbarians the dignity of the Roman because they cannot bear barbarous indignity among the Romans. Although these Romans differ in religion and language from the barbarians to whom they flee, and differ from them also in personal cleanliness and clothing, nevertheless, as I have said, they prefer to bear among the barbarians a worship unlike their own rather than rampant injustice among Romans.
>
> Thus far and wide they migrate either to the Goths or the Bagaudae or to other barbarians wherever they may be in power; yet they do not repent having migrated. They prefer to live as freemen under an outward form of captivity than as captives under a specious appearance of liberty. Therefore the title of Roman citizens, at one time not only greatly valued but dearly bought, is now repudiated and evaded, and it is almost considered not only base but even deserving of abhorrence. What could be clearer proof of Roman wickedness than the fact that many upright and noble men by whom Roman citizenship should be valued as a splendid and dignified state have been driven to such a state of mind by Roman cruelty and wickedness that they no longer wish to be Romans? Hence even though do not flee to the barbarians are forced to be barbarians. Such is the condition

of the greater part of the Spaniards and not the least part of the Gauls, and indeed of all those throughout the whole Roman world whom Roman wickedness has compelled not to be Romans.

Again, the Western Roman Empire fell because economic structures of inhabitants failed to be maintained and strengthened. The military activities of the Franks were the result of the fall of the Roman Empire, not its cause.

The strength of economic structures, then as now, makes our world.

THE ECONOMY IN A NEW LIGHT

Your finances are the subject of your individual situation. Every individual has his own set of circumstances. Together, the combination of all the individual financial and economic situations becomes the overall economic system of the community, country, and world in which we live. If we want to have a sound overall economy, we must ensure the health of the individual subeconomies that are part of it. This combination is the economic system of which we are a part.

America's economic system has successes, flaws, and paradoxes. These often are difficult to understand since what we have been taught often differs from what actually happens.

Let's begin looking at them, starting with your personal economy.

SOLUTIONS, PROBLEMS

We often like to solve things quickly. This is not a sound policy. As an example of what can happen, we can follow the process of "solving" the marriage penalty problem in our Internal Revenue Code. The problem arose to begin with when certain states mandated that income earned by one spouse was actually earned by the effort of both members of the marriage. The reasoning was simple. The wife took care of the things that would have interfered with the husband's ability to work; one person took care of personal matters while the other earned the money. This concept was called community property. By dividing the income between the two spouses, each half rated a lower tax rate than if the income was in one person's name.

People in states that did not allow "community property" had to pay higher rates of taxes because of this difference, so the first solution was made. Without looking at the reasoning behind the community property laws, the federal government simply extended the rule to all states. Single people who had to do both the personal things and earn the money now paid a higher tax rate than married people. Still no one looked at the reasoning behind the original problem to offer a solution.

The new solution they offered was a new tax rate that reduced the tax for single people. No one had looked closely at the reasoning behind the law so that there would be a solution, and this new solution created a circumstance where spouses working for approximately the same wages now were taxed higher than single people. A certain couple divorced in December, spent two weeks in Bermuda, remarried in January, and saved enough in taxes to pay for everything they did. Of course the IRS claimed it was a sham and did not allow it, but the opportunity was there.

Had the reasoning behind the community property laws been used to develop a solution, it would have been written that where two people supported each other, they had the right to share their earnings. This simple acknowledgment of the nature of community property would not have rested on marriage, and almost all the subsequent manipulation would have been avoided.

The best solutions are always found by understanding the problem that they are intended to solve. The issues described in this book is the place where these solutions are placed, and if the reader wants to turn to that section, he will find proposed solutions to a number of problems. Be aware, however, that understanding these solutions and how they work involves understanding the concepts behind them.

The section on individual economies offers no solution for a different reason. Individuals have to analyze their own situations if the solutions that are developed are appropriate to the problems encountered. There is no person in existence that has enough information about someone else's situation to solve their problems for them. This book's point of view is that there are certain elements in everyone's life that limit or allow solutions to develop. These elements are discussed with the hope in mind that each individual will be better enabled to make sound decisions that will make their lives more enjoyable.

PART TWO

YOUR PERSONAL ECONOMY

CHAPTER TWO

Making Money Is Illegal

A TEACHER ASKED his class why they were in accounting. One student answered, "Because I want to make money." The teacher responded that he would get a reward from the Secret Service for turning him in. "Making money," he said, "is known as counterfeiting, and that's a crime." We work for money. We connive for money. We gamble for money, but we don't "make" money.

What do you mean by this term anyway?

There are several ways to acquire money. We can marry it, steal it, inherit it, find it, or save it. These ways are important because we need money to accomplish most things. But money isn't the only way to reach a goal. We can use other resources to do many things without money. What I want to examine here is what we do to accomplish our objectives to fulfill our desires.

We use resources of all kinds to accomplish our objectives. Every person has to have resources to live. With money, we require more coming in than going out. We can't spend what we don't have and can't get. Somehow we have to obtain money, and we have to have something, a "resource," that we can give up to get it. How we get money and how we use it is the subject of this book, but the study goes further: how we get and use money relates to the way that everyone else gets and uses money, and vice versa. This interrelationship is called economics.

Economists try to understand the economic world by using models. These models look at the activities involved in economics as if they were some other process. Each model relates to some part of the economic structure of the world, but in studying each of these parts of the economic world, they tend to limit themselves to just one part. For example:

- Macroeconomics deals with the overall economic system and the procedures that keep it stable.
- Microeconomics deals with the individual company and how it maintains profitability.
- Demand economics deals with the time between when a transaction occurs in which there is an exchange of resources for money and the time when a transaction occurs in which there is an exchange of money to accomplish an objective. The purposes and insights are different.

In order to make the model work, economists are required to assume many things, but assumptions should normally be avoided. Assume can be spelled to read that it makes an "ass" of "u" and "me" and implies that anyone making assumptions can wind up looking foolish. Unfortunately, nothing in economics can be understood without assumptions. If it were not for assumptions, there could be no time for anything else. There are theories extrapolated from data that can never be fully developed and understood and must be explained by assumption. If it were possible to have all the facts, there would be no need to assume anything. Theories are tested regularly (and are basically sound) within the scope of their interests, so economic models using assumptions are ordinarily useful. Because the very nature of the available knowledge may be limited, it follows that studying them will give limited results.

Most economic models look at activity as a snapshot at a particular point. These models can be compared to balance sheets. These points of view try to stop the picture long enough to understand the situation as if the situation did not change. The problem is that in economics, you cannot assume that anything stays the same from day to day. The idea that any manufacturing process will remain useful over a period of time is one of the fallacies that cause people and businesses to fail financially and economically. Buggy whip manufacturers had a sure market at one time, and they are still sold at race tracks. With the invention of proliferation of automobiles, however, the maker of buggy whips has to know not only where and when buggy whips will be used, but in what quantity. Balance sheet thinking does not work.

IS SOMETHING VALUABLE OR JUST SCARCE?

Economics is not just the study of the distribution of scarce items. That is one of the assumptions that many economists make in their models. A quick practical look at the economic world, however, will tell you that scarcity has little to do with value. Plutonium and selenium are scarce commodities, and if scarcity was the controlling factor, people would be spending a great deal of money to acquire them. Instead, they spend a great deal of economic activity to control plutonium and find uses for selenium. Scarcity applies as a limitation, through price, where a good or service would be useful in accomplishing an objective.

On the other hand, wheat is relatively abundant, yet continually retains some value. Wheat provides the basis for making bread and initiates the action of eliminating hunger. This is clearly activity in the economic world. That concept—action—is what economists study; the nature of the product that the activity is concerned with is secondary to the dynamic of that activity. Scarcity, while it is important in determining price when demand already exists, cannot be the controlling factor in economic study.

Scarcity has another concept. It is a limitation, not an encouragement. Limitations are needed when harm can ensue form an action, but limitations never, in themselves, accomplish anything. An example of the devastating effect of a limitation is the attitude of the church during the Middle Ages toward charging interest on loans. When they labeled interest a sin, church officials limited its use to those who were not part of the church, usually the Jews. Thus, economic activity was hampered by the lack of a ready source and mechanism for funding projects. They undid themselves by handling over the "banking" activities to non-Christians, and it cost them more in the long run to get money. Since the Bible clearly states that interest is not a sin and Christ berates the man with one talent or coin for not giving the money to bankers so that He could receive his own with interest, the church's prohibition must have come from another source.

Over a thousand years earlier, the ban on "usury" arose from a very real situation that devastated the Western Roman Empire just before its fall (as appeared in the first chapter). But the excesses of the Roman bankers were met by the excesses of the people solving the problem, and the people suffered for many years because of both. As the poet Piet Hein wrote in Grooks:

When People start to plan,
And make up value systems,
They often choose as opposites
Stupidity and wisdom
But among wisdom-choppers
It's accepted, with avidity
Stupidity's true opposite
Is the opposite stupidity.

We sometimes admire the people who place the limitation of scarcity on products that are needed for economic activity. I heard a story about a surveyor in Ohio who found land available when he had money to buy. After many years, he owned well over a thousand acres, much of it farmland that he had no way of using. Since he owned it, no one else could use it either. Then land that could be used rose in price so much that farmers could not purchase what they needed to grow crops, yet these farmers admired the surveyor! Why? Because he owned a lot of land that was scarce.

ECONOMICS IS ALL WET

There's a model for the whole of the economy that can be compared to hydrology. Hydrology is the movement of water—from rain, streams, and rivers to oceans evaporating anew and returning to vapor so that it can rain again. To study of clouds is a good idea, but unless they are considered part of the overall system of the nature of water and its relationship to the world, clouds cannot be thoroughly understood.

Economists face a similar circumstance.

If the economy is to deal only with the flow of money downstream, as measured by transactions, it is like dealing only with moisture in the liquid state or water. Such a point of view in hydrology must assume that water follows its natural cycle and moves from moisture in clouds—that arise from a water source on land or ocean—and completes the cycle by falling as rain that becomes the headwaters of streams or rivers or back to the oceans. This assumption gives a limited view of water and what it can do, nowhere describing its versatility or intrinsic power. To understand the totality of the hydrological cycle, we must study these actions that we normally assume. The same problem arises in economics. Some economists have limited their interests to monetary economics and have failed to notice that there are many parts of the economic world that do not deal with money at all and are part of the natural order of economic activity.

Gross national product and other measures of the wealth tend to deal in terms of money. Wealth, however, is not actually related to that famous index. A person who has no money but is capable of providing all his needs by resources does not need more. He is no less an economic entity than one who must receive money and must spend it. Charles Dickens wrote of the concept, and W. C. Fields as Mr. Micawber delivered it in the movie of the book David Copperfield. He said that by having one dollar or, being British, one pound more outgo than revenue, the result is "misery." I might expand that to say, happiness translates as feeling sufficiently wealthy, and misery translates as feeling impoverished. Realistically, wealth must be measured by this criterion.

Needs are the elements that are required to accomplish an objective. There are at least two classifications of needs that can give us insight into the ways that needs influence the economic activities of people. The first involves twelve considerations (such as reality, coordination, etc.) that will be discussed in detail later.

The second involves developing priorities. Earlier we discussed Uncle Hascue and Aunt Flora in terms of priorities that influenced which needs they would fulfill. Abraham Maslow's book, Motivation and Personality, deals with a hierarchy of needs and refers to just such a prioritization. First, in terms of that hierarchy, Flora made sure that there was food in the house, or what Maslow called survival. Next they canned and preserved for future use what they would need during the rest of the year, or security. Then they established relationships with their neighbors through their church or belonging. After that they took care of the children (family). When these things were done, they beautified their home or created personal fulfillment. This prioritization leads to consequences in economics that affect demand curves of various products.

MONEY AND WHAT YOU BUY WITH IT

Many economists consider that the transaction with money is the sole basis of the economy. The nature of transactions, however, is not that they are an exchange of one item for money, but the exchange of one thing for another. When there are at least two people involved in an exchange of things and these things are exchanged directly, this concept is called barter. But an exchange does not require two people. I can exchange money to hire a housekeeper or keep the house clean myself. Here I may use money to have someone else vacuum the floors, but I also may use my time to do the job myself. I can get the same result as if I had used money, but money has not been used. Money is a part of the resource of an individual, but in turn, it is a result of a transaction when something of value was given up for money. If we measure the economy only at the point at which money exchanged hands, we count the value of a transaction that involves money twice, but do not count the same transaction at all when money is not exchanged.

There are two reasons that economists do not spend time on anything other than the observation of money transactions. How do I value the mowed yard if all it took was my time to mow it? We must understand the nature of value and the difference between a quantitative amount, as illustrated by money transactions, and the valuation of a nonmonetary transaction. Without the understanding, economists are forced to overlook the other parts of the economy that do not involve money.

The nature of value is such that its dynamic action cannot be made stable or consistent. At breakfast, an egg is valuable. You might be willing to pay quite a bit to buy an egg then. At ten in the morning, when you are in the field, have no stove, and are not hungry, an egg has no such value. The egg is not wanted. Values arise momentarily, and once satisfied, they disappear and have no "being." The very volatility of value makes measuring the values involved in a transaction impossible unless only money transactions are included.

The reason is that nonmonetary transactions do not have pragmatic value. You cannot go to the store and trade any nonmonetary value. Nonmonetary values have a life of their own. Sometimes nonmonetary values die instantly. The Hula-Hoop both rose and fell momentarily in value. When it lost its value as a novel toy, many stores could not sell their supplies of them. The transaction—a consumer buying a Hula-Hoop—required a fixed price that had the appearance of measuring value even though that idea of value was false. Without value, Hula-Hoops were unusable and unsellable. Values are momentary, transient, and frequently not understandable, but where transactions occur and money is exchanged, they become visible.

WHAT ARE VALUES?

While values are momentary, transient, and frequently are not understandable, they do have certain consistent characteristics. One of these characteristics is that values are limited by the resources available. If a person has a need for an item in twenty-four hours, yet has not spent forty-eight hours of his own time to acquire it, value cannot exist in his eyes. At all times, values are dependent upon using available resources in exchange for the item that is valued. Values exist only in exchanges, but no exchange can take place if the resources available are insufficient to make the exchange. In turn, values are the building blocks of demand.

One way of saying this is, "If your outgo exceeds your income, your upkeep becomes your downfall." The limitation of available resources is real. But at the same time, there is a subjective limitation that can govern this limitation of value. If I believe that I will receive a million dollars, I may ignore the limitation and make an exchange of resources for the thing I want. If, on the other hand, I have many resources but choose to believe I have none, I've put a ceiling on this limitation even though I actually and realistically am able to go to a higher limitation. Perceptions tend to control economic activity until reality becomes obvious. Often, reality is not accepted even when it is obvious.

Values are personal. If a person (for instance, you) has a financial note of bond that is quoted at $120,000 and yields 10 percent, you would receive $1,000 each month from this investment. Suppose that at an auction, you are lucky enough to buy a house for $50,000. The value you need to assign to it will not be $50,000, but in terms of what use the house has to you—$120,000. If that house replaced a home that you rented for $1,000 a month, you have been using all the proceeds of your bond to pay the rent. As a homeowner, you now have no rent. (For simplicity, we are ignoring such costs as utilities.)

To replace what you spend on rent, your value in the house is $120,000. If you buy the house at an auction for $50,000, and someone offers you $75,000 five minutes later, you should not accept the offer. Instead of having a $25,000 profit ($75,000 offered minus the cost $50,000), you would actually have a $45,000 loss ($120,000 value minus what you received, $75,000). Your cost in purchasing the house has no relationship to its value to you. It has also no relationship to the value that anyone else may have in the same item. The value that the possible buyer would give you bears no relationship to the value you should place on the house.

Price and past purchases have no meaning when you value an item. Many people feel that a store should use its historical value in inventory in pricing what it plans to sell. A can of peaches cost the store 25¢ and was priced at 30¢. While it was on the shelf, the replacement cost from the supplier rose to 35¢. You would have five-cent profit on historical cost, but have a five-cent loss on an actual basis. Historical cost is an accounting term and has no place in economic thinking. To return your situation to what it was before the transaction would require that additional outgo. This reflects an economic loss.

Values in any transaction are not the same for either party to the transaction. You may be willing to sell your time to a factory for five dollars an hour. The factory would not be buying your time. They would be buying the results of what of your activity accomplished during that time. If your job was to package products, and you could pack fifty items in an hour, the value of an hour of your time to the factory is fifty times packaged for five dollars (your pay rate). If another individual could package one hundred items in an hour for the same amount of money, his hour would be half as expensive for the factory as your hours, or five dollars for one hundred items.

Because values are personal to each individual and each transaction, each party to the transaction must determine two points of reference: first, he must set his own value, and second, he must determine whether the transaction can occur or not by reference to the value of what will be given up to the value of what is received. Each transaction then is made up of different individuals having a different value for each item in the exchange—but finding that each one's value for what he will receive is more important to him than what is being given up.

Values, though, are not related to the item valued. This may seem to be a strange statement. If you have two identical pencils, and someone is in need of one to write down the telephone number of a beautiful blonde, he may be willing to pay you $10 for your pencil. Thus, the value of that pencil is $10. However, if there is no one willing to pay that amount and you had no use for the pencil yourself, you may have to accept five cents for the second identical pencil or give it away. The two pencils are identical, but until someone puts a value on it, the value of the pencil is not related to the pencil itself.

Identically, the $10 value was random and momentary, and you need to be somewhere else when the buyer realizes it. It will only take a short time before he realizes that the value he had placed on the pencil was excessive. Values exist for only a moment in such cases, and he will not take kindly to your "cheating" him.

This idea gives us a clue as to what the real nature of value is. It shows us that the value is the ability to satisfy some unfulfilled objective of the person who is doing the valuing. The understanding of the need, wish, demand, or any other word used to signify a fancy or inclination is essential to better understanding what makes economic thoughts and actions known. It is important to understand that an objective may have many different possible characteristics.

Demand is the combination of values that apply to a specific item. While value is specific to an objective, demand relates to all the items that can be substituted to accomplish that objective by everyone who has an objective that can be satisfied.

For example, if you want meat for supper, you may have the choice of beef, chicken, pork, lamb, or turkey. If you dislike one of these meats, the demand for that particular meat is reduced, but the overall demand for all meat has not changed. Value and demand both relate to the objective, which is the controlling factor in developing economic activity.

CHAPTER THREE

Twelve Keys to Getting Anything Done

THERE ARE ALWAYS things that affect what you want to do. These things are called factors. When these factors are ignored, you cannot accomplish what you want to do. You are locked out. The key to unlocking a factor is first to recognize it, and second, adjust your goals to accommodate it.

There are twelve considerations that must be addressed in solving any problem, including an economic one. These considerations are divided into related ideas and begin with the following:

1. Coordination, reality, action, and objectives—the four considerations that provide energy and follow accomplishment.
2. Things, locations, knowledge, and relationships—the four that inhibit any solution.
3. Acquiring, using, protecting, and disposing—the four that describe the actions that allow economic activity to proceed.

Let's take them one at a time.

Coordination removes impediments. We need umpires, rules, understandings, contracts, and laws to give us reference points for working together. Fulfilling the need for coordination may require nothing more than allowing the person coordination in an activity to function effectively in the role. Even when there are more people available for the job, there must be one person in charge. Coordination requires that there be one source of reference with the full ability to coordinate all the activities around it.

Only one source of coordination will work. Second sources or systems working together with primary coordinators cause such confusion that value cannot be established. For example, the conflict in the country that was once Yugoslavia destroyed the ability of the people to rely on one-source coordination. All economic activity was destroyed in that case. Croats wanted to coordinate all activities in accordance with their principles. Moslems and Serbs tried to do the same. There was never a final mediator or judge who was acceptable to all factions. Without the coordinator, no one could determine what was to be done.

Similarly, both buyer and seller must be coordinated in time and place—having the same understanding of the situation at the same time—for an exchange to be successful. To do this, they must have a common source of references. If there is a competing source of reference, there will be confusion, and coordination will not exist. The value of coordination not only decreases, but actually disappears if the number of coordinators exceeds one.

Reality is another basic principle. It requires that a person not use resources in an unreal and unnecessary way. Reality requires that living creatures eat. There is the story of a man who had a horse he tried to wean from eating, but just when he believed he had succeeded, the horse died. A skewed reality told this man that a horse could live without food, but death is another reality. Every action that is accepted as useful must have a basis in reality. But reality has to be the reality that is perceived to be useful, and it must be authentic to be effective. American foreign policy assumes that everyone accepts American values of compassion and benevolence and how those values are expressed. These values are often unacceptable to other people and are perceived by them as quite the opposite of their intent. The resulting disagreements are confusing to Americans because their inability to understand conflicting values places them at odds with their compatriots on the planet.

Action is required to accomplish anything and may require a different valuation. To get another person to do something may require money, favors, or some other type of value. At different times, punishment and slavery were used. Action requires a threshold of resources and an objective to be useful. Without a minimum amount of resources, people become unable to act. Inaction creates boredom. Boredom and action are opposites. When people are bored, they may act irrationally just to avoid boredom. Additionally, the inability to think about the consequences of an act may be used by some as an excuse or justification for acting irresponsibly. We read about such mindless, unjustified acts all the time, including the one about two girls in Akron, Ohio, who vandalized their neighborhood with paint. Their excuse was "We had nothing else to do."

Objectives may or may not be easy to come by. A person with no objectives will simply relax into inaction and accomplish nothing. Typically, everyone has objectives. The frustration of not being able to accomplish any objective is the drive that causes people to take action and produce economic activity. That frustration as a motivator will only be effective if the action overcomes it. True boredom that cannot be overcome alienates people. The result is often a revolt against the cause of the frustration.

The nature of an objective is so important that we will deal with it separately later. No economic activity can occur without its involving an objective, so it will be a constant part of everything that follows.

Denial of basic threshold resources, such as the security of daily living, and the knowledge that they have some control over their lives by Israelis caused the Palestinians to realize that their efforts and activities are going to be frustrated in any case. They believe it is better to be dead in such a situation, and many act accordingly.

Without purpose, goal, or objective, nothing has value; without action, there is no value. Reality means that value must fit into the structure of the economy, and without coordination, values are lost.

These four concepts are controlling concepts, yet none of these directly involve money. Advertisers have to provide an objective and get action. An individual has to decide what is real in his own perception of reality. Coordination allows different perceptions to cooperate. And the overall purpose defines the rest. These are controlling concepts of economics but are seldom studied and seldom understood because monetary economic activity is the principle economic interest. The valuation of the next four qualities of locations, things, knowledge, and relationships typically are related to objectives, as we have seen before, and are all necessary for accomplishment of objectives. Each of these has a different method of being valued.

These second four concepts are about limitations that restrict any economic activity that might have been considered in the first four concepts.

Locations both in time and space have finite values and are limited by supply.

The academic and practical side of economics usually deals with these, the second four of these twelve principles. "Locations in space and time" are finite. To build a thirty-foot boat in a twelve-foot basement would be an exercise in futility. To try to do a forty-eight-hour job in twenty-four hours without help would be silly. There is a finite amount of these factors to be used to accomplish the main objective, whatever that objective is.

Each day we have a maximum of twenty-four hours, some of which must be used for rest and recreation. There is a direct relationship to locations in time and space that limit us in all we have to do. These limitations give us a type of economic value that could be called rent. Rent is a catalytic factor. Action occurs over, in, or through a location, but the attributes of the location are unchanged.

For example, rent pays for the use of an apartment, but when the lease is up, the apartment is available for someone else. Whether you use your time or kill it or create something in it, the time is gone, in any case. The nature of a location is such that it is there and may be used—or not used. Whether used or not, the location exists independently of its economic use. If the objective is assumed, the demand is derived from it, and the availability of the location becomes critical.

Things have a different type of valuation. Where scarcity of things applies, more can be manufactured. Yet things are not finite. We can make, manufacture, or buy many things that can be used to accomplish a purpose. Things, therefore, have a different type and characteristic of economic activity. Supply and demand are necessary for rents because there is a limited supply, but commodities—things—are less limited. Here the supply will increase to meet the demand and typically is dependent on demand. At any one moment, the supply may be fixed, but over time, supply will rise to meet the demand. Typically, things have a separate cycle of life that does not parallel the financial cycle, but will touch it only at the point where an objective is satisfied.

Gravel in the ground has no value. Gravel mined has only the appearance of the value of what it cost to get it out of the ground. The value of gravel on a driveway will encourage people to pay for it. (At this point, when the payment is made, there is an interaction between the production cycle of the gravel and the financial cycle.) Over time, gravel sinks into the ground again and becomes valueless because it is no longer usable.

The cycle of production starts with no value. By activity, it develops value, but at the same time, it becomes valueless again. Cotton in the field has no real value. Picked, carded, woven, cut, and sewn, it becomes a shirt. The shirt is paid for in an economic transaction, but since it will eventually be worn out, it develops a negative value. It must be disposed of. After its disposal, it has no value again.

Knowledge becomes part of the overall makeup of the person who learns it. Once knowledge is attained, it becomes a resource and demands no more expenditure of other resources.

Knowledge is an entirely different type of necessity relating to an objective. Until a woman knows how to sew, she will not be able to make a dress. She can learn how to sew, but when she has learned, she no longer needs to learn. She has the knowledge.

College education, training, school learning, and vocational learning all have a similar investment necessity. It costs so much to learn to teach. Once that is learned, with updating and maintenance, knowledge retains its value as a resource. However, actual payments—which are the transactions measured by economists—are no longer needed. There is no need to spend money on what is already known.

Relationships are resources that allow families, partnerships, and other combinations to exist. Relationships are essential to human activity. Mother and daughter is a relationship. Father and son is a relationship.

Obtaining these relationships normally does not involve financial activity, but social dates cost money, contracts may involve lawyers, and book sales require advertising. As relationships become more complex, maintaining those relationships require significant use of resources. Christmas and other greeting cards help us to maintain our relationship with other individuals.

Activities such as sports, work, and casual play provide means by which relationships can develop.

Communication is essential for this development, and to communicate, people have to start together from a common point. The phenomena of Michael Jackson, Elvis Presley, Frank Sinatra, and other such megastars have economic value because these stars provide a means by which people can continue to refer to common interests.

Language is a matter of relationships as well. There is a story about an American who was visiting Monaco. He had a good accent for the little French he knew and asked a street sweeper, "Est-ce que un vie a la chemin superieur?" (Do you know a way to the higher road?) To his chagrin, the sweeper launched a five-minute spiel in French. Only when he pointed did the American find any meaning in his talk. The American could not understand a word of his response—communication was cut, and they could not relate by language.

Without the ability to understand one another, relationships cannot exist. This goes beyond the simple misunderstandings in a local setting. Without understanding our relationships to each other and to the world and specifically by choosing to limit those relationships—such as in Serbia, Croatia, and Bosnia—we destroy economic activity.

Value usually relates to one of these four concepts, things, locations, relationships, and knowledge. Each of these categories of goods and services has its own style of valuation and creates its own demand curve.

The ability to acquire, use, protect, and dispose of what is available may create other means by which value is determined.

Acquiring what we need is essential. We must acquire a purpose so that life has a meaning to us. Without purpose, nothing has value. We look at acquisition as obtaining things, but any of the elements that are missing need to be acquired. Acquiring sales for a company involves salesmen and an advertising campaign. Acquiring goals for a student involves providing schools for children. Acquiring knowledge of economic reality requires accountants.

Without action, there is no value. Acquiring action then becomes essential. Political activists, whether misguided or not, are attempting to move people into action. Salesmen again want action by the buyer and determine their success by how much action they have acquired. Acquiring anything necessary for the accomplishment of objectives becomes an economic activity.

Use of what is acquired is essential as well. Shoppers who, on impulse, buy food that they allow to sit in the refrigerator find that they must acquire more income to replace the money wasted. By using all that is acquired, buyers can reduce their needs for funds.

But objectives, action, and all other concepts must be used as well. Action spent accomplishing nothing does not advance any objective. Objectives that are fuzzily explained cannot be accomplished. Reality that is ignored or not accepted creates loss. Using what is available and acquired makes it possible to accomplish what is intended.

Protection also requires understanding. Protection of an objective is a subtle concept, but one that can make or break its accomplishment. Real estate developers often move into an area and start building without consideration of the residents nearby. In almost every case where this has happened, the neighbors have fought the developer. To protect their investment, these developers needed to prevent obstacles from arising. By explaining what is being done and the options available to these neighbors, many such fights have been avoided.

Protection also has its obvious meaning. Homeless people keep everything with them and avoid having anything that other people would want to steal. But more often, protection means not inciting the types of anger that create danger. If my doing something will cause another person to want to harm me, I can choose to do it or not. I do not want to corner the tiger if I am hunting because animals and people will fight back when cornered.

The last of the twelve important concepts is disposal. We often hear stories of elderly people who have only enough space in their home to walk to certain areas or sit down. They have saved everything all their life and now no longer have any place to put more. Taking out the garbage is essential. But we also need to dispose of old objectives, unprofitable actions, and beliefs that, in reality, do not reflect what exists.

Many parts of the "rust belt" have places that are known as brownfields that are so contaminated, they can no longer be used. Reclaiming what is worthless is part of disposal. Disposal can also involve efforts to eliminate waste at the source so that properties do not become brownfields. Current packaging processes that produce too strong a package need to be reviewed so that less waste is produced.

Of the twelve considerations, the first four are controlling concepts, yet none of them involve money. Advertisers have to provide an objective and get action. An individual has to decide what is real in his own perception of reality. Coordination allows different perceptions to cooperate. And the overall purpose defines the rest. These are controlling concepts of economics but are seldom studied and seldom understood because monetary economic activity is the principal economic interest.

The academic and practical side of economics deals with the second four of these twelve principles. "Locations in space and time" are finite. Things are not finite. Knowledge is an either/or situation. Once acquired, it does not need to be learned again. Relationships are intangible assets that make life more possible.

Acquiring, using, protecting, and disposing are ways in which all the other concepts are made to work.

These twelve concepts are central for economic activity.

THE FIRST DIGRESSION: OBVIOUS VS. IMPORTANT

Some readers may feel that the previous discussion is obvious and doesn't have to be stated. Many times we pass over an idea, not because we disagree with it, but because "everyone knows that." The fact that something is obvious does not mean that it is unimportant, and some obvious ideas need to be restated so that their effects can be observed and understood.

There are three reasons people confuse obvious with unimportant. First we genuinely believe that we know the idea. For example, an author who was proficient in the software program VisiCalc refused to take lessons in Lotus. Years later, he found that the two computer programs were completely different and that Lotus would have done him more service. He had wasted time for years doing things the hard way.

The second reason is that there are only so many hours in the day, and we do not want to waste time on the obvious. This reasoning is rational, but it leads to ignorance of subtle effects of ideas that are obvious. Time is an important resource, and understanding the effects of things that appear obvious wastes that time. Ordinarily there is little difference in the effect of not pursuing more information about an obvious subject. This study of demand economics, however, has found that there are significant important consequences that result from certain obvious facts, and these are a major part of this study.

The third reason has to do with our wish to "get on with it." Grade school students want to do addition and subtraction, but tend to overlook the proper formation of their numbers. Later, they may confuse threes with fives, sevens with twos, and fours and nines. Never being sure of what they are working with, they constantly make errors and usually form mental blocks about math. Had they worked on the basics, they would have been able to overcome their error-making even before it became a problem.

These two concepts, obvious and important, are completely independent of each other. That we need air is both obvious and important. That the sky is blue is obvious, but not very important. That a person is left-handed is not always obvious and also not important. The fact that a certain stock on the stock exchange is going to rise is not obvious, but is very important to the trader. To overlook something because it is "obvious" is to close our eyes to what it can mean.

One of the most important discussions in this book is the role that objectives have determining demand. Without objectives, there will be no demand, but the fact that objectives are important is obvious. For this reason, prior perceptions about objectives should be set aside to allow understanding of these concepts. The new and old concepts can be reconciled later.

There will be other ideas in the rest of this book that are obvious, but also important to understanding the premises. Consider the analysis and recognize the consequences before dismissing an idea just because it is "obvious."

BACK TO THE SUBJECT

Economic activity is not necessarily monetary activity. Monetary activity, if we use the hydrological model, is like the rapids in a stream. As long as there is value flowing downstream, the monetary activity is realistic, but what happens when value no longer exists because there is no longer any value flowing downstream? Such a possibility occurs in depressions and requires our understanding.

ORGANIC ECONOMICS

Toilet tissue paper is normally found near toilets. The tissue paper that is available today is not the same paper that was there last year, yet last year, there was tissue paper in the same place. Such a product is part of the economic structure of the owners of the toilet. Almost none of the items in use today were there last year, and even houses and automobiles are replaced at different times. Such is the nature of organisms, and economic structures follow the rules that apply to organisms.

Organisms are complex and include many suborganisms. The human body is an organism and is comprised of other organisms called the heart, the lungs, as well as many other organs, glands, bones, and systems that are clearly defined, each doing its own job to keep itself and every other part of the body functioning. In just such a manner, your economic activities are part of the overall economy. What you (and others like you) contribute and what you (and others like you) claim are the basis of all economic activity.

The study of economics is the study of activity. There can be no activity unless there is something that is active. Hydrology is the study of the activity of water, but that study would not complete without an understanding of what becomes wet. The economic entity requires some study as well. Every person ingests and eliminates food and waste every day. So does every economy take in and expel. Every other process that the body does can be compared to an economic activity.

Economic entities have the same characteristics as organisms. A retail store receive goods, displays them, and delivers them, but the store itself is little changed by this activity. The store is an intangible entity that is evident by its physical attributes. Even the fixtures that constitute the physical attributes of the store change over time—a store has a birth, grows old, and dies, just as a person does. Yet the store remains as an economic entity throughout the changes that occur during its life.

The activities of the store are not always financial activities. Fixtures may be removed from stock and placed on display. Personnel may contribute to the store's success without being paid, especially by a manager giving it more of his time. The store may contribute to charity, allow its premises to be used without payment. Many store activities are not included in the financial records of the company. But there is one inflexible rule: no store can give out more that it has or can get. This gross transaction limitation is one of the most inflexible rules in economic study.

Every individual is, like the store, an economic structure. Each has resources and develops needs and uses for those resources. These resources, needs, uses, and activities tend to be repeated over and over. They tend to have a stability that lasts until circumstances change. Marriage, a new job, a move to an apartment, and other activities will cause a change, but the individual develops stability again until the next change. The understanding that every individual is a stable part of an overall economy is essential to an understanding of our role in it.

When Elizabeth I's England defeated Philip's Spanish Armanda, her sailors were kept on the ship in port and allowed to die so that the fleet would not have to pay. English merchants took advantage of this situation and smuggled in untaxed merchandise that undersold merchandise made by the Spanish workers and put them out of business. Spanish merchants did not have and could not get the cost of their merchandise and taxes as well. The gross transaction limitation put the Spanish merchants out of business.

A similar situation is in effect in the United States in the form of Social Security, as we will see later.

With the collapse of the business interests in Spain, the normal economic cycle could not continue. As a result, Spain, Mexico, and other countries had to turn to a different type of an economic activity. In Spain, this was based upon the relationships of the hacienda owners and the peons. Coordination of activity required that the peon do what the hacendado told him to do. Mexican economics continued with the hacendado system until the Mexican Revolution in 1910—a revolt against the excesses that the hacendado system allowed. By concentrating all the land to growing crops that the owner could sell, there was no land left for peons to farm. To survive, the Zapatistas, who were one of the revolutionary groups led by Emiliano Zapata, had to reclaim the right to use the land.

INCOME AND OUTGO

In economic structures, income must exceed outgo. This is the financial concept. The clear understanding of the requirement that resources exceed need—the economic concept—does not mean that resources have to greatly exceed needs.

To study most economic entities, we must use the economic concept. Monetary economies are actually very rare in most parts of the world and in most times. Because of the surplus of resources in the equatorial jungle, the necessity for trading between different members of the community was never a problem. In the local languages of Bulape, Congo (formerly Zaire), there is no word for house or food. Shelter is easily manufactured from palm leaves laid one over the other, and food grows profusely. The economic requirements to satisfy the needs of these people rest not on material items but upon relationships. Income and outgo are expressed through relationships rather than money. To this day, the people of Africa are more concerned with a poetic mastery of language and a clear hierarchy of relationships than they are about acquiring material goods. When material goods were made available to them in the terms of money for gold or diamonds, they used these materials to establish status in the community. By giving access to the elements of status to many people, coordination is lost, and war is frequent. There are those who feel that this is an argument for class structure, but this is not a book suggesting any organization as ideal. That people need coordination to establish sound relationships may call for different solutions in different situations.

Other economic possibilities were illustrated in the book Roots by Alex Haley. The author described the economy of the Mende people of western Africa, which was based upon every individual having a specific role in the community with a specific job to accomplish. Each person over the age of eight was assigned a traditional job. At eight, each child started guarding the goats, and at twelve, they cared for the cattle. Every different age had its role, and these roles changed until all the roles needed by the community had been handled by each one at a different stage of life.

In Russia, the Boyars owned the villages. These villages, known as mirs, had a requirement that every individual contribute to the good of the community. The village was required to provide the Boyars with so much grain, and the exodus of any individual from the community jeopardized the village's ability to live up to its requirements. Fearing the loss of its young people meant that the village would do all in its power to prohibit their movement from one village to another. Serfdom continued to exist because the established relationships required it. The villagers were more concerned about loss of labor than the Boyars. The legalities followed the customs.

The mir accepted the requirement of loyalty to the Boyars because at one time, Russian peasants were captures regularly by Petchenegs—nomadic people of the Turkic family—and other barbarians from the steppes of Central Asia. These barbarians sold the Russian peasants as slaves in the Byzantine Empire. Fear of being captured and sold as slaves was so strong that the people of the villages were willing to support a military force four times larger than western countries, such as France, that had far greater population. They were also willing to support a system of serfdom.

HOW IMPORTANT IS THE OBJECTIVE?

If the objectives create value and value determines demand, objectives are important to the economist. The objective of an accountant is to represent reality. Usually, accountants do not accept any information that is not backed up by some concrete information. The puffery that salesmen use to make sales has no value for the accountant. A manager who wants action to accomplish a purpose will not value the beauty of an artist's painting while he's in action mode. Each objective determines the value of everything related to it.

Objectives come in all shapes and sizes. If a gang tells a storekeeper that they will destroy his front window if he doesn't pay them graft, and the storekeeper wants to prevent the loss, then his objective becomes protecting his window. That objective may be accomplished by calling the police or destroying the gang, but the possibility of these alternate solutions is a major factor in determining whether he is willing to pay or not. Normally, a person will choose the solution that will work and that will use the least amount of the resources that he has available to him. What action is best for the shopkeeper? The expectation that he can destroy the gang is so remote that there is little reason to expect him to use that solution. Calling the police will be used only if the storekeeper perceives that they will be able to protect his window. If the storekeeper considers that the threat is real, his desire for protection becomes one of his objectives.

Objectives have lives of their own. Photographers know the value of having their cameras ready at the moment they observe a beautiful or newsworthy sight. If the photographer is not expecting a picture, he will not get his camera ready. If he does and is ready, he makes a picture. The moment arises and disappears quickly, and if the situation has not been expected and prepared for, the picture is lost.

In physics, there is a distinction between active movement of a substance in the possibility that the substance may move in the future. Water behind the dam, still, has no motion, but it has the potential to have motion. Similarly, money in the bank is not in motion but has the potential to be in motion. All it takes is a signature on a check. On the other hand, water flowing below a dam is inactively moving. It is said to have kinetic energy. When the check is written, the money also becomes active. This distinction between potential activity in money and kinetic activity is important to remember. It is never essential to spend money just because you have it.

Impulse buying is a concept that grocers use to increase their sales. The buyer is shown how the product will satisfy some likely objective, that product is placed where the buyer will see it as he passes, and usually the buyer will, on impulse, buy it. If the product is not shown to satisfy some objective, however, the buyer will not pay any attention to a display of products or advertisements for them and will not make the purchase.

Objectives also have different characteristics based upon categories. Objectives of coordination require that one and only one source of authority be allowed. Objectives of reality require constant review and recording. Objectives of action require accommodation with the preferences of the worker.

When more than one source of authority exists, coordination is impossible. Under the warlords of Afghanistan, the expectation that people will cooperate with each other becomes remote. The effort of each warlord to become the sole source of authority destroys the ability of the people to live in peace. Each warlord has the wish to be the most important person in his area if the boundaries of his area are not fixed. Time and effort is spent in establishing supremacy that could be spend on providing what is needed for more important objectives.

The stability that comes with cooperating with reality shows another category of objectives. Accountants have the objectives of assuring their readers and the users of their work that the information they use is real and not just a pipe dream. Arthur Andersen's demise (one of the long-lived prestigious accounting firms) is not because its people did not work or because they did not do the job assigned to them. The value of their signature lay in its ability to guarantee reality. After the Enron scandal, it became clear that people no longer perceived that their imprint did so.

Objectives involving action are a different category as well. Accomplishment of most objectives requires obtaining action. Often people want things done their way, and when there is difficulty having someone do it their way, they react by saying, "I'd rather do it myself." Efficient businessmen, however, recognize that there are only so many hours in a day. By defining what is needed by encouraging other and by assuring that workers are supported, not condemned or exploited, these managers are able to obtain cooperation from those they work with and obtain the action they need from their workers. Many times the result of this cooperation is large corporations, all dedicated to the same objective and involving many workers.

Objectives have different characteristics, depending on the nature of what can be accomplished. If the objective is to establish realism in a physical world (registration of deed for properties, for example), it requires that great deal of time be spent on covering the minutiae of every part of transaction (such as a real estate sale). The value of the work of a title company is based upon the accuracy and thoroughness that assures that there will be no contest about the land after it has changed hands. Similarly, the value of the accountant's work is based upon how well the readers of his report can be assured of the validity of his presentation.

Objectives of action require a different set of criteria. Teeg, a friend's dog, fits this model. Teeg was a black-and-white dog and got his name form the word integration. Black and white together. Each morning at 9:27 a.m., he went to the door and waited for it to be opened. Once it was opened, he went south into the sagebrush near Taos, New Mexico, and disappeared. At eight minutes after eleven, he would bark at the door to be let in. He was seen to come back from the east every time. He had established a pattern of action.

Most people deal with purpose and action in just such a rhythmic fashion. Where the only change in climate is the daily cycle, as in Central Africa, that rhythm is short and basic. Where the changes include seasonal change as well, longer cycles give a different attitude toward action and more variety in the actions of people.

On the other hand, if action to avoid boredom is the goal, a different situation occurs. If entertainment is the goal, a performer needs to be confident, loose, and easy. Neither accuracy nor reality is needed to perform as a comedian. A party host has the objective of making people feel at ease. In these circumstances, a relaxed, confident air is essential, even if the host is penniless. We cannot expect that a salesman makes an accurate, precise, and exact representation of the physical properties of his product if he is selling a dream that involves the imagination of the purchaser. That dreaming means a complete change of every part of the purchase, and the nature of such real things, such as the furnace in the basement, is irrelevant. Whatever the goal, the value of any activity or thing, is directly related to its ability to accomplish the goal.

Objectives may or may not be stated. Analysis of actions often shows that objectives may not even be recognized. When asked why pro-life movement did not have more emphasis on making the life of the mother better so that she would not want an abortion, the reply was "That would be too hard, and besides, it wouldn't get people worked up." The presenter failed to notice that the objective of preventing abortion was secondary to the objective of obtaining both action and coordination. Here, the activities of the pro-life movement show that the stated aims of the organization do not correspond with the observed aims.

There are several reasons for believing this. Laws that prohibit actions do not apply if the circumstances create a situation where obeying the law is impossible. Underground doctors, who are not registered to begin with, are able to make far more income from clandestine operations than from legal procedures. Prior to Roe v. Wade, the prevalence of dilation and curettage (D&C, a standard medical procedure) was frequently noted. Since that decision, the procedure is far less prevalent. The procedure had the effect of an abortion, but was not illegal.

Determination of the objective of an economic entity is not necessarily to be found in the stated aims of the entity. Whenever the actions of an individual, family, organization, partnership, corporation, or any other economic entity or structure does not work toward the stated aim of the entity, you can analyze the actions of the entity and find that a different goal is really their interest. People do not support objectives that do not produce results that they accept or tolerate.

Such support is not necessarily in the form of money. Social clubs frequently have balance sheets with negative net worth. The purpose of the club is to provide facilities where people can gather and enjoy themselves. Plumbers who are members often fix the plumbing without charge, and other members contribute to the continued existence of the club. Balance sheets of such clubs often show negative net worth, yet their existence is never imperiled.

Objectives may be direct or indirect. Working in a factory for money to buy food is indirect to the primary objective for eating. Buying a camera is an indirect objective to a photographer whose direct objective is to take a picture. This distinction plays a major part in the phenomenon of substitution. A photographer originally made his pictures in daguerreotype. Each time a different process that made photography easier was refined or invented, the photographer abandoned that process for the newer one, but the primary objective remains, and still is, the photograph.

Indirect objectives can be found in many layers. The farther each layer is from the direct objective, the more instability affects the economic health of the structure. Such a situation would mean that makers of paint pigment will need to be more alert to the color changes in new cars than the paint makers, who will need to be more aware than the painters, who will need to listen to the salesmen and the engineers who are directly in contact with the buyers and designers.

The direct objective remains unchanged. The indirect objectives are constantly changing. A typical shirt, for example, may have customer, salesman, buyer, sewer, weaver, thread maker, and cotton grower, among others, as the layers needed to produce a shirt. A change in preference from cotton to polyester will change some of these layers. A trendy change of color will affect others, but the owner of the shirt will continue to wear clothes.

No economic activity can occur without some objective involved. Seemingly, random acts are often found to have roots in some objective. A woman whose father died while she was a teenager may feel that he abandoned her, and as result, her objective is to punish all men because of her feelings. That objective seems irrational, but it exists. The objective may not be understood, even by the woman herself, but the objective is there. When the girls we mentioned before vandalized cars and homes with spray paint in Akron, Ohio, were confronted, they said that they were bored. They vandalized property with the objective of escaping boredom.

A real failure in our educational system is the idea that children are sent to school to give parents the freedom to work. The teacher then is a disciplinarian whose job is to control the children. In this case, control create boredom, anger, or frustration, and the incompatibility of the children's objective—to learn rather than to avoid boredom with a substitute parent—with the teacher's objective creates a real disciplinary problem.

By this time you will notice that everything is "obvious" and would seem to be overly spelled out, but let's look closely at the points covered so far:

1. Every individual is an economic unit in the overall company.
2. The health of the overall economy depends on the economic health of each individual.
3. Economics is defined as the study of activity.
4. The unit of measurement of activity is value.
5. Demand can produce scarcity that affects price. Scarcity does not create demand.
6. Value is the ability of a resource to accomplish an objective.
7. Money is first a reference point or benchmark for value.
8. Value is related to the purpose and unrelated to the thing being valued.
9. Price and value are distinct and not related.
10. Economic structures have resources and outgo.
11. Wealth is the difference between income and outgo.
12. Outgo can never exceed resources.
13. Transactions can occur without money being involved.

14. In a stable economy, statistics may represent the economic situation but are incomplete.
15. Values are the result of objectives and limited by resources.
16. Historical cost has no place in economics.
17. There are twelve considerations to accomplishing any objective, and they are the following: objective, coordination, action, reality, things, locations, knowledge, relationships, obtaining, using, protecting, and disposal.
18. Every individual is an economic structure.

CHAPTER FOUR

Have You Got What It takes?

WHAT IS MONEY?

IN CHAPTER 2, we noted that "making money is illegal," so what is the reality behind the idea? Money is required to accomplish many objectives. People may not work for you unless you pay for them, and many things that we need require money to purchase them. But where does the money come from? Factory workers exchange their time for money. Mine owners exchange ore or metals for money. Salesmen receive money as commissions for accomplishing a goal for making a certain number of sales that has been agreed upon or getting such an agreement. Teachers receive money for conducting classes. Money is a return for giving up resources. We will go deeper into this later.

THE SECOND DIGRESSION:
EXISTENCE OR JUDGMENT?

Although perception is more influential in economic activity, actuality is more important in understanding this book. It's critical to look at the actual situation rather than the situation as it could, should, or ought to be. Many people feel that if the situation is "bad," it doesn't exist. When the idea is in control, people are hurt by what they refuse to believe.

Pedro Carbajal is a lardon (thief) on the streets of Mexico City. In order to eat, he has to become a lardon, and he is good at it. Frequenting the cambios (where money is exchanged and checks are cashed), he picks his mark and ingratiates himself. If he can, he lures the mark to a secluded spot and robs and may kill him. If the mark will not cooperate, his fast pitch makes the mark pay him anyway.

We may call his way of life reprehensible, label him a thief, and eventually put him in prison, but for this study, we are not concerned with what ought to be, just what is a fact. Pedro's resources are his knowledge of the city and his past patter that gets results. With these resources, he acquires money and uses the money to acquire the things that satisfy his objectives. What Pedro does can be labeled as "bad," but such badness does exist. Many things that we detest have a real effect on our lives.

The other side of this problem is that people have, in the past, taken a theory or another's justifications as their own reasons for doing what they do. Machiavelli's The Prince was a description of the power politics of his time, pivoting on cunning, duplicity, and bad faith. French kings, among others, used the book as a justification for whatever they chose to do. They did not recognize that it is the objective that is important and not the method when methods are acceptable. By justifying their actions with the idea that what they did was done elsewhere and also appeared in Machiavelli's book, they could ignore the fact that their methods were not in the best interest of their people. This is not an acceptable use for this study. The best use of this study is to take it as a basis for observation of the world around us. By seeing our surroundings in a new light, we may better understand them.

This study does not attempt to deal with the right or wrong of any of the concepts. It is only interested in things, systems, and processes as they are. Because it will accept ideas that are clearly wrong, it is not advocating or encouraging what is wrong. Encouragement of anything is not an objective of this book. Its objective is to look at life as it is and accept it as it is. An alcoholic cannot respond to treatment if he continues to assume that he is a different person than he really is. An economy cannot rectify its problems if it continues to believe they do not exist.

BACK TO THE SUBJECT:
CONTRIBUTIONS AND RESOURCES,
CLAIMS AND NEEDS

Resources are resources because they contribute to the accomplishment of some objective, whether for the person involved or for others. On the other hand, a right to use a resource constitutes a claim. Eventually, all contributions are equal to all claims, but current contributions often need to be matched to future claims. When time is used by someone to accomplish his own goals (as in mowing the lawn), the match is instantaneous. With two or more people, this becomes more difficult. Children exchanging time spent on homework for the parents taking them to a movie can be considered the children's contribution of time and a claim for movie, so money isn't absolutely required. Often, quid pro quo comparisons between contributions and claims exist without notice. Where relationships are the essence of the transaction, most activities are completed without a conscious recognition of the transaction.

The normal transaction, however, uses money to allow matching claims with contributions over time. Money is used to represent past contributions during current transactions. The value of money changes with contemporary resources and needs. At any one time, all active contributions will equal all active claims. Unless a contribution is available for use as a claim, it has no value as a resource. This is true because we have defined both contributions and claims in relationship to each other.

It doesn't help to have claims without anything to use them for. Money itself does not feed the hungry or allow you to see a movie. There has to be food to eat or a movie playing at a theater. If there are too many claims against too few contributions, each good or service has to be increased in price to establish a proper balance between all the claims and all the things that can be bought. The total money supply of all the people at a specific place and time must match the total of all the goods and services that are wanted and available at the same time to the same people. This is the ideal situation, and when it occurs, it establishes stability. When it doesn't happen, the economy involved loses its stability and becomes chaotic.

When Germany printed money prior to World War II, the situation become chaotic. At the same time, as the money lost its ability to be a reference point for value, it was said that it took a wagonload of money to buy an armful of groceries.

That said, the claims against an economy (resources, sometimes represented by money) that are available and ready to be spent must match the goods and services (contributions to the economy) that are available to be purchased. This balance is achieved when people are willing and able to contribute to the economy. This contribution is not the same as work. The Puritan Ethic says that if you don't work, you don't eat, but a contribution can take many forms. Loans of money for others to use, being a dependent child or unemployed mother, or coordinating the efforts of others all qualify as contributions, but may not qualify as work or a job.

Resources become resources when the value assigned to them is made available for use in accomplishing some objective (a contribution), either for the owner or for some other person. To be of use for someone other than the owner, there must be an exchange for money or something else of value (a claim). While that exchange may involve money, the something being exchanged may be another item. Charity giving can be for a good feeling. A mother preparing a meal may be for the maintenance of the family relationship, as is the father's payment for schooling. Apprenticeships are served for the knowledge they develop, and management of an apartment house may be for rent.

Claims against the economy are the other side of the economic exchange. Charity recipients find themselves unwilling to participate in the charity because inherently, they expect an obligation will be developed. Children accept meals and the schooling because they feel those are part of the relationship. Apartment managers expect to retain control of apartments because they have met their obligations. The most significant claim against the economy, however, is represented by money.

Claims are significant at the time of exchange. In physics, this separation of active (kinetic) forces from possible (potential) forces is a major consideration. It has the same nature in economics. If you build a house, once the house is complete, the only economic value would occur if the house is rented. The existence of the house provides an economic value only in a theoretical sense if there is no economic activity associated with it. But there is a potential economic value in the ownership of economic claims.

Contributions to an economy may be represented by jobs. An individual (paid by the hour) contributes some service that is valued by his employer (unrelated to the time involved). But contributions are not limited to jobs. Entrepreneurs may perform any number of services that are paid for by the general public or some part of that general public. At other times, the public pays for the service or the good through taxes, or subscribers make the payments, such as the breadwinner in a family who pays for the survival of the children.

Contributions are the other side of resources. Resources are to be found only where needs can be met—that is, when objectives can be satisfied by using a possible item—or when value is perceived in the eyes of those who control what could be part of a transaction. Uncle Hascue and Aunt Flora, noted in a previous chapter, are examples of keeping objectives within their resources and thereby reducing needs. Most economic activity, however, occurs when value is recognized by another possible player in a proposed swap.

The value of a typical service, such as advertising, lies in two parts of this situation. By increasing the perception that objectives can be attained—that is, finding and revealing what can be done with an item—the perceived needs of the prospective buyer are increased, and value is perceived where it was perceived before. The second attribute is that the buyer is informed about the location and availability of needed or desired items. Here, value is increased because of accessibility of the item.

In other words, resources are resources because they contribute to the satisfaction of proposed objectives. This shows the interaction between what is given up by contribution to the economy and the resources of the individual economic structure that makes the contribution. Clean clothes are essential to individuals interacting with others. The objective is that interaction. The resource for obtaining the clean clothes can be the time and energy of the wearer. Most people, however, prefer to use a cleaning service or dry cleaner. The contribution of the dry cleaner involves an exchange of the dry cleaner's efforts for money or another tradable substitute for his resource. The dry cleaner is making his contribution and thereby developing his resources.

Contribution to the economy is not a general thing. Rather, it is a specific thing. A contribution from any structure may be given to any other specific structure that exists within an economy. A job involves the exchange of a resource on a regular basis. That is also one of the definitions of a contribution. Some jobs provide resources for individuals. Others provide for government entities. Every economic structure can use the contributions of others if it has the resources available to make the exchange.

A contribution does not require that a person have a job, however, nor does it require that the contribution be paid for. Mothers contribute to the survival of the species. Usually, the contribution of a mother as a mother is not paid in money. Mothers who choose to make their contribution without obtaining the necessary resources to fulfill their objective are a problem in any society.

Contributions may be supported or not. Economically, value only occurs when objectives are supported by the willingness of individuals to support transactions. Sometimes people do not have the resources to do so. When they do not, they are often unwilling to make a contribution.

The depth of the Great Depression was not caused by indolence. People were willing to work for food. The gold standard had been dropped, and labor had become the backing for the dollar. However, labor was not valued, and most people had only labor to contribute. Recognizing this, the government established the CCC and WPA programs, both to obtain objectives for individuals and to give value to labor. The value of labor was not established, though, until the years of World War II. The long and sustained growth that occurred after World War II occurred because the minimum wage had established the backing for the dollar, and more importantly, it gave a sustained value to that minimum wage.

Over time, the natural result of stability (we will discuss this in a later chapter) allows potential economic contributions to concentrate in the hands of fewer and fewer people. The Puritan work ethic (let those who do not work not eat) creates a very difficult situation when contributions are accepted only for "work." As more and more of the possibilities for contribution are held in the hands of fewer and fewer people, those who are no longer able to contribute find themselves outside the economy. Once outside, they have a choice of starving or finding some way to obtain claims, not unlike our aforementioned Mexican ladron. When society fails to recognize their situation, their response when they choose to live is theft, scams, robbery, and other acquisitive crimes.

Society can recognize their situation in various ways. The Bible calls for tithes. These tithes, economically, provided for a transfer of funds from the workers to those in need. Social Security provides for transfer of claims from workers to those who cannot work. Relief and welfare do the same. Each of these programs recognizes that it is essential for the continuation of economic health that all people be included in the economy. Recognition that recipients of these "transfer payments" are contributing to our economy by avoiding an impossible situation is an important understanding that everyone should acknowledge.

There is always a balance between contributions and claims. This works best when the balance is stable. When more claims (money) exist than goods and services, each claim will become less valuable until the balance is reestablished. This is one example of inflation (more on this shortly). Increasing the claims may work to increase available goods and services when individuals are below the threshold that allows people to contribute. A doctor's clinic in a poor neighborhood, for instance, may be able to exist because people have contributed money from elsewhere. But if, as in Medicare, the increase in funds is placed in a circumstance where goods and services cannot expand, the result is a sharp increase in costs without any comparable increase in value. Medical services are provided by doctors, but medical schools have resisted training more doctors. Medical supplies are under patents, so supplies are artificially limited. Yet more and more money is spent on the same available supply of medical services.

TYPES OF RESOURCES

Many sources of money are not easily identified. Both nonworking and working wives receive money because they are cared for by their husband. Bond holders receive money because they can clip the coupon from the bond. Thieves receive money because they take it from others. Protection racketeers receive money because they have frightened their "marks." Politicians receive money because they can influence the coordination of laws. Prostitutes receive money for renting their bodies. All these sources of money are resources for the economic structure that receives them.

Resources, however, are not limited to things that can be exchanged for money. Earlier, we noted that having the objective of a mowed lawn can be satisfied by hiring someone to mow the lawn, by doing something for another person in exchange for his mowing the lawn, by requiring a son or daughter to do the job, or by taking the time to mow it yourself. Resources do not have to be turned into money.

An instructor in an investments class pointed out that there are a number of ways to acquire money to invest. He listed these: marry it, inherit it, steal it, find it, or save it. Of these choices, he said, only "saving it" is generally accepted by the general public. But what does "saving it" mean? The difference between the price you receive for the resource you give up and the price you pay for the sum of all your purchases is still available to be spent. That difference—resources less expenditures—equals savings.

As we discussed in chapter 2, a resource is what you can give up in exchange for something else that will accomplish some objective or objectives. It does not become a resource until you consider it a resource and choose to relinquish it. The actions of the muscles in your lungs are a resource because you can choose not to breathe. Children have been known to turn blue having temper tantrums until they pass out and no longer can choose. When you choose to breathe, you make the action of breathing a resource.

A breath is not an expensive transaction. We do it all the time. The air that we breathe is free for the inhalation, and we do not need to spend money or any other resource on the act of breathing. However, when emphysema creates an inability to breathe, the alternative (sometimes portable oxygen tanks) costs money. While rational people usually choose the least expensive resource to give up for an objective, there are some hypochondriacs who choose to use oxygen tanks even though they are capable of breathing. Their objective, in this case, seeking sympathy or quelling an irrational fear of suffocation, causes them to relinquish a resource for the oxygen tank. The oxygen tank has become a need.

Resources must either be more valued by others or less valued by us. A golfer giving up his time to play a round of golf has determined that his time, as a resource, is less valuable to him than the joys of playing the game. Here the resource given up, time, is less valued than the game. A factory worker, on the other hand, receives money for his time, but the amount of money received must be enough to overcome the alternative uses for his time. Sometimes people do not pick up pennies when they find them on the street because the effort of bending down to pick up a penny is more valuable than the penny itself.

Resources come in a variety of types. They can be found, stolen, traded, be claimed against others, be by-products, techniques, inside knowledge, and many others.

Gold is a resource that sometimes is found loose, lying on the ground. The forty-niners found gold in the creek beds of California. If those prospectors recognized what it was (and not fool's gold, which looks the same), the gold was there for the taking. Many men prospected for this mineral, and a number of them became rich. By being rich, however, they became targets of others who either hadn't found any gold or who chose not to look for it. These people acquired what they wanted by stealing from or exchanging other resources with them. Gold was used to trade for other things that people needed.

One of the interesting developments in these gold fields was the fact that the miners who found the gold and panned for it were not necessarily the ones who ended up with it. Women who fed the miners and otherwise took care of them accepted gold in payment. Since the price was usually set by the cook, the miner's gold often ended up in the cook's hands. Found resources have a tendency to follow this course. During the time before the Armada and following it, Spanish gold ended up in English merchants' and German bankers' hands.

We read earlier in the first digression how Pedro Carbajal used his ability to steal as a resource. Other types of resources include a relationship as a dealer with a manufacturer or other supplier or a relationship with a mother and a child. Resources can also be abilities, talents, or knowledge, such as the ability to choose which supplier will get the business for a purchasing agent, having an ear for music for a piano tuner, and knowledge of the current values of stocks to a stock trader, and many, many more.

As resources become more available, as gold in California, they command fewer claims from others. During the gold rush, the value of the gold declined as the quantity available increased. There is a rule that "available claims will always counterbalance available contributions." This means that as more gold was found, more gold was required in exchange for available supplies and services. This process is called inflation. Inflation is not the same as increase of value in a specific item while other items remain at the same price. To be considered inflationary, the price of every item must advance at the same rate.

An example of the nature of inflation can be found in the change of the minimum wage from $1 to $1.60 during the presidency of Richard Nixon. The increased wage rate caused workers to receive more money to spend. During the five-month period following the increase in the minimum wage, all prices went up. The price level after this period was 60 percent higher than before the change was made.

Resources become income in exchanges and outgo when they are used. As a result, the flow of resources is opposite to the flow of funds. The resources you give up become a contribution to the economy, and in their place, you receive claims against the economy. Usually these claims are represented by money, but there are other claims that are in different form. Some of these forms are stocks, bonds, property, and relationships. Quid pro quo exchanges call for future favors. Support in political races, however repugnant, calls for favorable response to future requests. There are many other resources. These serve only as examples.

Stocks are claims against the future income of a company and a resource to the owner. They are issued after an exchange of money for them. The stocks themselves are intangible representations of a relationship between the owner and the issuer. Stocks are speculative since their value is not directly related to any tangible thing; they relate to an intangible relationship similar to the relationship of a parent and child. The parent earns money, and the child spends it. Similarly, a corporation earns money, and the stockholder spends it. If the company makes a profit, it is possible that some amount of money will be paid to the owner based upon the results that are applied at the time. If the company does not do well, there is no value in the stock.

Bonds also are resources to their owners, but these claims against the issuer have a set amount that is required to be paid in a fixed time period. These claims have been set up by allowing the use of the owner's money, or some other claim, by the issuer of the bond. Credit cards are similar resources. Here the value of the resource is dependent on the promise of the user to repay the amount at some future time. There is faith on the part of the issuer that the user will be able, and will, repay the amount spent. For these reasons, issuers verify past credit information so that there will be reason for such faith. As a person has acted in the past, he is likely to act in the future.

Resources can include private property. Shelter can be obtained by rental of an apartment or owning a home. Private property is based on the right to use an object without hindrance from others or obligation to them. In different cultures, the definition of private property varies since they recognize private property differently from ours. The British and the Americans believe that someone must own everything. If the property is not owned by an individual, then the government owns it. However, in Sweden, Swedish forests are not owned by anyone, including the government. The Swedes have free use of the forests, but assume a responsibility for caring for it. Africans generally assign ownership only when an item is ready to be used. If it is not in use, anyone can use it. A Spanish land grant was given by the king for the purpose of supporting the owner so that he could fight in the king's cause. The Spanish in New Mexico lost their land because paying property taxes on it was foreign to their culture.

Because private property can be used without hindrance, it is available as a resource so long as there is a recognized objective that can be accomplished by using it. When ownership causes a person to maintain the property when there is no such use (as in an old home, when it is necessary to move away and there is no buyer or renter available), it changes from a resource to a need. Since resources must be used to maintain the home, that objective takes away from the resources that could be used for other purposes. Things, goods, services, or anything of value has this dual nature.

Where money is used in a transaction, the flow of the resource from seller to buyer is exactly opposite the flow of money from the buyer to the seller. While the flow of money from hand to hand eventually returns money to where it started, the flow of resource value is a linear progression from no value, to value, to no value again. A resource may be increased in value by investment before the transaction occurs that allows it to be considered a resource, but unless there is a goal that the resource can be used for, that investment is wasted.

UNDERSTANDING THRESHOLDS

There is a threshold of required resources before a person can be a part of the economy. Homeless people live below that threshold. To find work, a person must be at a location where work exists and must show a presentable appearance to a possible employer. Homeless people are not in a position to do either. What few possessions they have must be guarded, or they will be lost. The employer is not likely to appreciate an applicant who appears for work carrying everything he owns with him. There can be no rational expectation that employment in a regular job can be a possibility in this situation.

The idea that money will help in this situation is difficult to support. These people are "outside the economy." People who are outside the economy must have resources to survive.

Sometimes these resources include such things as the knowledge of which heat vent is most comfortable on a frosty night, or which cop on which beat will look the other way. Food is a special problem. Since there is no ability to warehouse, these people develop resources to find food or starve.

Some resources are repugnant to society. Stealing from grocery store shelves should not be condoned, but may be the only resource available to such people. Some restaurants put out partially eaten food from customers or the day's discards for foragers.

Money is not a resource to a homeless person. Having money in his position exposes him to the danger of being robbed. Any money that is available to such a person is usually spent as soon as possible to avoid this problem. For a homeless person, until a threshold of resources is significantly increased and achieved, he's still outside the economy. Until a threshold of resources is achieved, economies and cutting costs are of little use.

LIVING ABOVE THE THRESHOLD

Since life below the threshold of economic participation is difficult, once a person has moved to a place above that threshold, he becomes protective of that new environment. People who are near the threshold do not take risks of any type, nor do they attempt to allow change. When people have surmounted a threatening economic situation, they want to ensure the higher threshold is secure. Hillbillies from West Virginia who were able to get jobs in Ohio during World War II supported unionization most strongly. These Hillbillies as a group of people were the least likely to accept change, even change for the better. For them, the most important objective in life was to avoid the chance of dropping back into a situation below the threshold. The fear that this will happen influenced every economic activity that they became involved in.

These people are also the most generous to those who are below the threshold. More contributions to assist others (as a percentage of available resources) come from them than any other group. Because they understand the situation and because they would want to receive assistance if they were themselves in the more difficult environment, contributions are in a larger proportion of their expenditures.

When such people move to a higher level of resources, they typically are unable to adjust to the requirements of maintaining themselves at that level. Stories of lottery winners who quickly go bankrupt are representative of this. Since they start out having few resources, unnecessary and extravagant spending and purchases are tempting, and the limits inherent in the larger amounts of money are not understood.

Normally, however, this fear of loss is persistent, even when they have earned, won, or acquired more resources. The reality they perceive about having more is colored by the experiences of their past, and they do not want to risk being pushed out of the economy. This attitude is an expectation that the balance between resources and needs will never become even and that resources will never be enough to assure that they will always be safe.

LIVING WELL ABOVE THE THRESHOLD

Others live on a level far above the threshold.

When the balance between resources and needs is perceived to be sufficiently positive, people are willing to risk loss in the hope of gain. Such people tend to be careful about money without feeling threatened by the possibility of loss. At some point, they even feel that they are able to purchase whatever they want without considering that there will be consequences. Most people aspire to be living in such a manner that they do not have to worry about spending as they would like to, but the need for claims against the economy is limited. Claims are the basis for the valuation of resources. When they are undervalued, resources become limited, and goals become less and less possible.

DIFFERENT DEMAND CHARACTERISTICS

Since resources are the ultimate limitations on demand, we can conclude that each of these types of resources result in a different demand curve for the same product. For example, there is little demand for any economic activity in groups outside the economy. They have no ability to store anything, they have few economic resources, and what resources they have are a threat to them.

In the second group, where resources and needs are delicately balanced, the people have needs that are inflexible. Typically, all the needs they choose to fulfill are consumption spending, such as food, shelter, clothes, and occasional splurges such as movies. In the small amount of difference between their resources and needs, they can be influenced in their choice of expenditure. Paradoxically, they are extremely subject to scams because they feel that any hope to improve their resources would be an improvement. Lottery tickets are especially attractive to such people.

After several attempts to improve their lot, these people become extremely careful about taking any risks. Any threats to the remaining resources that would mean they are likely to return to or become part of the first group suggest that risks of any type are extremely dangerous to their economic situation.

By keeping their preference for consumption goods as their resources increase and avoiding risk, these people are more inclined to be influenced by advertising. Their consumption patterns increase, and their demands become flexible and include more items. These are the mainstay of the consumers' market.

The third group, with a positive resource-to-need ratio, is not subject to influence in the same way as the middle group. Being used to risk, they are less driven to experiment with proposals that are scams. They tend to determine their own uses for their resources and have fewer losses from impulse actions.

People pass through these groups in different ways. Some children are born in poverty and belong in the first group as far as money goes, but feel that their resource on time is unlimited.

They spend their time as if it had no end. As they feel that they can always work later, they are unreliable workers. Some do not feel that working is all that necessary. They also have a positive resource-to-needs ratio since they have few needs. As their obligations and needs grow, they adopt a more responsible attitude, but still hold a place only in the second group.

Other children who have been born in a higher group still have a profligate attitude toward their time and waste it. If they are not schooled properly about the value of money, they tend to overspend and fall into the lowest group. Not having learned how to make and save money, these people can end up homeless as often as any group.

There are also individuals who have money and have the discipline to care for it. These people are not subject to whims and will only be influenced by reason.

HOW AVAILABLE ARE RESOURCES?

Historically, the ratio of resources-to-needs has varied in the overall economy. During the Hundred Years' War, English resources from looting in France were very extensive. Everyone had something of value in their home. But times changed. The French ousted the English, and the resources of the nation were limited to their own country. With everyone wanting the limited resources, fights and contention broke out, and the Wars of the Roses continued for the next eighty years, until everyone was weary of the instability.

With the mood changing to a demand for stability and peace, the Tudors were able to support a despotic monarchy. Elizabeth I even had Shakespeare on the carpet for threatening the peace when he included something in one of his plays that she disliked. The prosperity of the Tudor period increased resources. Later, the Stuarts allowed the resources to be used up. As resources declined, the contention of the Wars of the Roses returned, and the king was executed. This cycle is a consistent theme in history throughout the world.

MONEY, PRICE, AND VALUE

Some resources are resources only because they can be used in a particular way. Time is often a resource, but can be used only when applied to other resources. If there is no market for an individual's time, it may not have any value as a resource. Mexicans in a little town near Taxco, with no resources and no economic activity, had time in plenty, but no way to use that time, except for procreation—which has a separate set of resources that do not interact with other resources.

Money is a "medium of exchange." This term is frequently used in economics but seldom thoroughly explained. Resources that have limited usefulness and are applicable only to specific objectives can be exchanged for money. That money is then accumulated and exchanged for resources that, in turn, allow satisfaction of different objectives. (Here we need to remember our second digression. Issues of morality are not a valid concern in economics or in this book.) Prostitution is a means of exchanging a sexual resource (usable for only that particular purpose) into food, shelter, and other things that allow attainment of other objectives.

With money, then resources can be utilized that otherwise would be wasted. The use of money allows accumulation and quantification of the resources that will be used to satisfy a large number of different objectives.

Money has another purpose. In colonial Virginia, tobacco was easy to grow and always had a definite demand from tobacco addicts in England. Everyone had access to it, and it frequently changed ownership regularly. Because it had a known value and was easily transferable, it became a type of specie, or coin money, in the colony. It would seem silly for a planter to send tobacco to England, have specie sent back, and then return the specie to buy items in England. The colonists would find it much easier to have an account with a bank in England and pay for their purchases in England with withdrawals from that account. Tobacco served as a replacement for specie in the colony, and everything worked well until Parliament required English specie for essential documents. Since there was little specie and less interest in acquiring it, the Intolerable and Stamp Acts struck at the very basis of economic activity in that colony.

By having a clear standard of acceptance, each citizen in Virginia knew how much value he needed to place on his tobacco in comparison to every other need. By using tobacco as a stable reference point, he could determine the percentage of his resources that he would need to assign to every other purpose.

In turn, his relationship with every other Virginian could be determined because the community accepted a common valuation for tobacco. Tobacco as specie, like all money, was a benchmark to use for the valuation of each objective for the individual and also a benchmark for interaction with the larger economy. Specie is always backed by a commonly accepted commodity.

To become specie, the chosen commodity needn't be designated as such. It must have a value that is perceived to be nearly constant, be readily available, be easy to divide, and readily transferable. Tobacco served all these requirements. Gold, silver, and many other commodities have served as specie in the history of man. Specie makes it possible for all goods and services to have a common reference point. Within the framework of an individual's mathematical scissors, specie allows an individual to determine what amount of resources he requires to accomplish all his objectives and determine whether those objectives can be accomplished or must be dropped.

Externally, specie allows common references between people as to the nature of price. Remember, value and price are not the same. As a factory worker, I value my time in reference to the amount of resources the factory will pay for that time. As a factory manager, I value the time I pay for in terms of what the factory worker accomplished during the time that I bought. Value is a relationship of the thing acquired to the objective for which it was acquired. Price is the common designation of an amount established in a specific transaction.

Value, then, is a matter that relates only to the person doing the valuation, as in this case. Adam had an inn, and Bob wanted to buy it. Adam, as the owner, valued the inn according to what it would take to replace it. He had a place to live tax-free, his meals were provided to him, and he had an income as well. To replace these things, Adam estimated that he would need $200,000.

Bob, the buyer, valued the inn on its income potential alone. He already had a restaurant and another inn, so he had no need for the things that Adam valued, and so Bob valued the inn at $150,000. Of course, no transaction took place. Valuation is the comparison or what will be given up and what will be gained in a transaction. For each participant, the exchange must increase what he perceives to be his total resources. Value is always a comparison, and quantification would only apply as a means to determine which is larger. Mathematical calculations do not belong in determination of value, except to determine which is larger.

When large numbers of valuations occur, statistical inference can be applied. Statistical inference may indicate that a size 16/32 or 16/33 shirt has more value than a size 18½ 35–36. This comes about because there are more men who fit into the first size than the second. Individually, the value of each is the function of the size of the wearer. A man who wears the first size will not value the second size at all. A man who wears the second size will place no value on the first. The seller of shirts will place a value on each that relates to his ability to sell the shirts. The statistical inference will relate to the seller, but is of no concern to the buyer. Each participant places his own value on the item based on his own objective in acquiring the shirt.

There are three possibilities when a transaction is being contemplated, as with Adam and Bob. Adam valued the inn more than he valued what he would acquire if the transaction took place. He did not enter into the transaction. The second possibility is that Bob, the buyer, valued what he would give up more than he valued what he would acquire. Neither of these possibilities will lead to a transaction. The third possibility, that both the buyer and seller value what they will obtain more than what they will give up, does lead to a transaction, but the value is a range and not yet a price. If I value a shirt at up to $100, and the retailer will sell the shirt for anything over $20, the value of the shirt is a range of values between $20 and $100. Houses sell this way frequently. A seller will price his house at $100,000, and a buyer will offer $90,000. Negotiations then go back and forth, and the price will end up somewhere between those two amounts. Once the amount is set and paid, it becomes a price.

Prices have different characteristics from values. Prices are set. Values are ephemeral. If I offered $100,000 for some land, and the seller is asking $150,000, the negotiating range is between $100,000 and $150,000. When I discover oil on the land, my value becomes far greater than the top of the range. I do not change my offer, but my value has increased greatly. However, if I find something different that becomes more important than the land, I may withdraw my offer. The land no longer has any value to me. Values can change from moment to moment. Prices, which only exist after a transaction has occurred, never change.

Just as prices reflect only one point between two values and do not reflect the values of the participants before the transaction, so too prices do not reflect values after the transaction.

Earlier we discussed the home buyer who paid $50,000, but valued the home at $120,000, and the pencil seller who sold one pencil for $10 and another identical pencil for five cents. In both cases, the price had no relationship to future value.

CHAPTER FIVE

The Mathematical Scissors

THE "MATHEMATICAL SCISSORS" is a controlling factor in almost every situation. You cannot spend what you don't have and can't get. You cannot use resources that are unavailable to you.

A SHORT TRIP

Earlier in the book, we met Pedro Carbajal in Mexico City. Elsewhere in Mexico, it's the end of the dry season, and you're traveling from Mexico City to Taxco. You make a mistake and do not continue on the high road to Taxco, but find yourself on a back road through a dry and dusty area and go through a little town. There's no activity in the town. The cattle have bones showing through their skin, but the donkeys are better able to use the resources of the area. They are still fat and sleek. The ground is barren and dry, so dry that it would be washed away with the first rains. The grass has been eaten into the ground. This town has no resources.

The people are not active because they have nothing to be active with. Only the grass that grows behind fences still exists. In such a situation, people must export what they have, and since all they have is time, it's not surprising that these people are found working in the United States or on the streets of Mexico City, where work is available. There they can be active. That these people are what others call lazy cannot be disputed, but that they cannot be otherwise also cannot be disputed.

Failure to effectively provide enough resources to enable a person to contribute to his community has often made the idea that people should work laughable. The reality is that they do not have the resources to be active, not that they are "lazy." This blade of the "mathematical scissors" is not open.

No social security comes to this farm village; no funds of any type are available to people there. When you measure economic activity, you find that in such situations, there is none. Taxco, because it has silver mines and work for people, has expanded from 16,000 in population to over 160,000 over a fifteen-year period, but with no resources, there is no economic activity in this smaller town. Even in such cities as Mexico, the work has already been apportioned. When that happens, there is no work to be had. Even here, everyone must eat.

THE THIRD DIGRESSION:
PERCENTAGE AND ABSOLUTE MATHEMATICS

The third digression has to do with the nature of mathematics. Again, this is obvious, but because the application of mathematical principles affects economic activity so conclusively, we need to understand those principles. People study "mathematics" and feel that they understand the subject. Frequently, they fail to notice that "mathematics" deals with a number of very different subjects, such as counting math, accumulating math, percentage or fractional math, algebra, geometry, calculus, etc. By failing to separate these different subjects, they can attempt to use a rule that is valid in one type of mathematics while working on another type and fail to understand why their answer makes no sense.

"Counting" math, including addition and subtraction, has only one rule: every item must be distinct. The introduction of set theory under the "new math" was an attempt to improve math understanding, but it violated that one rule at the inception and created far more problems than it solved. By using set theory, a calculus concept, the "new math" allowed two plus two to add up to two, three, or four. For example, two Millers and two women could be two if both women were named Miller, three if one woman was named Miller, and four if neither was named Miller. The simple rule that you only count something only once was ignored. Counting math can add objects of any sort, so one 300-pound man and one 100-pound woman will count as two people. A method of avoiding loss while traveling is to count the number of items that must be accounted for each time you move. In this situation, a bag of soap, a purse, and a suitcase are each one item.

"Accumulation" math, multiplication and division, has an additional rule. Each unit must be the same as every other unit. Sometimes in the past, airplanes were not loaded by the number of people but by weight, since five 300-pound men have the same weight as five 100-pound women. Only when the planes became powerful enough to carry enough excess weight was this changed. Recently, an investigation of a small commuter plane crash was related directly to the excess weight at takeoff. Here, the common unit is a measured weight, the pound. This unit must be exactly the same for each unit in multiplication and division.

"Percentage" or "fractional" math does not use either of these rules. There is one unit: 100 percent, or some other denominator, but that unit can be anything under the sun. There are numbers of stories where misunderstanding percentages enter news stories and give false impressions of circumstances. In one year, Russia had a growth rate of 5 percent in GNP, while the United States had only 2 percent. Because of the difference in the base, however, actual increase in the United States was nearly twenty times greater than in Russia. Census records in 1980 showed increase in population of 38 percent in Henderson County, North Carolina, and 10 percent in the county next door, but because Buncombe County started with 170,000 residents while Henderson had 48,000, there were 1,000 more additional people in Buncombe than in Henderson. Percentages must be understood to be useful.

A news story in Russia once indicated that the Soviet track team had come in second in a meet, while America had come in "next to last." It failed to mention that there were only two teams in the meet and that "next to last" was a misleading way to say first. Such distortions come easily with failure to recognize the interaction of absolute math with percentage math. This interaction between percentage and accumulative math plays a vital part in the understanding of economic value. Understanding the "mathematical scissors" requires an understanding of this difference. Both expense and revenue are accumulative math, but the difference between them is percentage math. Both expense and revenue are based on the dollar, but the difference is based upon either the unit of expense or unit of revenue.

As these close toward each other, businesses are cut off from the possibility of being profitable and continuing to operate.

Algebra, trigonometry, calculus, all have different rules and different purposes. Just as in every other division of mathematics, each of these must be understood separately. However, these are not germane to this study.

Statistics is also considered a part of "mathematics." Statistics, however, are separate and apart from mathematics, while using some of the same terminology. There is never an "accurate" answer to any question involving statistics, even though our idea of math as being "accurate" causes us to look for such accuracy. Most economic studies use statistics rather than mathematics, and the mathematical terminology leads people to expect accuracy, which is never possible and not even useful.

Statistics became a study in a peculiar way. Before the American Civil War, every piece of clothing was individually made. Tailors were necessary and important workers in every town as there were no store-bought, ready-made clothes. The number of men called to arms during that war meant that soldiers had to have clothes made without access to the tailor. Uniforms were ordered to fit most men, and some clothes were too large and some too small. Different sizes, both larger and smaller, were ordered, and more men were able to get comfortable clothes. This process continued until there were many ordered sizes sent forward to the war zone.

The makers noticed that there were always many more uniforms ordered for the most average size and fewer and fewer ordered as the size varied from that average. Moreover, it became obvious that after thirty sizes were chosen, these size variances became stable. By going to a military unit and determining the appropriate size for thirty men, they were able to make suitable uniforms for several hundred. The first thirty "represented" the whole unit. This "bell" curve circumstance was a pointer to the study of statistics.

Statistics uses this phenomenon to draw realistic pictures of quantities that are far too large to be measured. The results of statistical studies are representations of the most likely appearance of the overall quantity being considered. Most conventional economic studies use statistics because, for their purposes, the information obtained is as realistic as it is possible to acquire without interfering with the operation being studied.

Statistics does have its limitations. Like multiplication and division, it must deal with a common unit (in economics, the dollar), and it requires a homogenous population. Statistics based on the weight of men and women together will not make any sense. Each population has its own bell distribution curve, and the men's curve would be different from the women's. To expect to clothe women based upon the men's statistics would be ludicrous. Such limitations, however, can be allowed for. This study does not use statistics because it deals in values, not prices. Values are not easily quantified and can quickly arise and disappear. In the logic of the nature of value, however, the difference between absolute mathematics (addition, subtraction, multiplication, and division) and percentage mathematics becomes critical. These two divisions of math become the blades of the "mathematical scissors."

BACK TO THE SUBJECT

The "mathematical scissors" consists of three parts:

- The first is the maximum amount of resources that we have available, either to use or to trade for something we can use. This is an absolute number.
- The second is the amount of resources we use or money we spend. This also is an absolute amount.
- The third is the difference between the first two. It is always a percentage.

This is how it works: Marge Blackwell lived in a town of many millionaires. She herself was uneducated and was married to a man whose mental capacity was limited. At times he held a job, but his ability to work was so limited that an employer lost money when he hired him. As a result, Marge was always scrounging to have enough to eat and care for her husband. Even with welfare, her income barely covered her grocery requirements. She had her house free and clear, but other expenses used all her available resources.

Word got around that grocery prices were about to rise by 10 percent. The millionaires in town rearranged their finances and easily allowed the increase to take effect. The "mathematical scissors" had a different effect on Marge. Now groceries had a new price in absolute terms, her resources were fixed in absolute terms, but her ability to pay was completely destroyed in terms of the percentage of her resources.

If you receive $1,000 per month and have vital needs for only $800, you have $200 to spend or save as you choose. On the other hand, Marge received $800 and needed $775. A $30 increase in groceries was no problem to the millionaires in town, but Marge could not overcome it. Her needs became $5 more than her resources.

No person can pay out more than 100 percent of their resources—that is the resources they have and can get. Therefore, the maximum ability to acquire any item by any person, business, government, or other entity depends upon the total resources of that entity. Resources are the perceived ability to give up something that is of value to others. The amount of resources is an absolute number. The price of any item also is the accepted perceived amount that the item commands. This also is in absolute terms mathematically. The ability to use resources is a percentage mathematical problem and changes each time either the resources or the price changes. Raised prices and lowered resources act as two blades of a virtual pair of scissors. When these are close enough, the buyer is cut out of the economy altogether and must look to other means to satisfy his objectives or abandon those objectives.

The mathematical scissors is critical when demand is studied. Objectives vary, and the objectives that are most important take precedence over others. When the most important objectives have a price that is near the value of a buyer's resources, other objectives are dropped. The different nature of various priorities leads to different characteristics in how they are considered valuable. If a person is starving, food will have first priority. Self-preservation in most cases has the highest priority, and people will hold on to what they perceive as their means of surviving, even when better and easier means to survive are available. Their knowledge of what will allow them to survive stops them from making changes unless the change is clearly understood. "First-level demand" is inflexible and difficult to change. If forced to make changes in their first-level needs, people will fight with every possible means.

(First-level priorities are expanded on in a later chapter.)

The mathematical scissors applies to every economic structure. All outgoes are a percentage of the income of the economic structure. You, as an economic entity, cannot spend what you don't have and can't get. Every absolute income increase or decrease and every absolute outgo price change changes the relationship of each outgo to the total income and all other outgoes. An increase in rent reduces our ability to pay as much for food, unless there is an increase in income. Every other outgo will also change as a percentage of income if there is a change in any one of them with a higher priority. When food as the first priority is priced at 100 percent of a person's income, all other outgoes are set to zero. As the percentage of resources needed for food becomes less either by increased income or decreased outgo, other priorities come into play.

The reason that the people of India are wealthier than the people of other countries is not that they receive more money. They do not. Their wealth (shown by their ability to spend more of the money they have on movies than any other country) is created by the absence of high prices for those things that are higher in priority than movies; that is, lower prices for necessities. They can survive well on an income of less than $1,000 per year.

In another time and place, individuals with far higher salaries are required to use money to repay previous purchases or otherwise pay critical charges and have no money left to use for personal enjoyment. An income of $35,000 with repayments and interest totalling $20,000, and rent, food, and transportation of $15,000 leaves less available to be used than the Indian example.

THE DEVELOPMENT OF DEMAND IN REGARD TO PERCENTAGES

The mathematical scissors creates a situation where all expenditures end up being a percentage of the total resources of the individual economic structure. There are examples in every activity. Some examples are clear, while others more difficult to see, but every economic transaction or exchange is part of the activity of at least one economic structure.

We can find a clear example of the workings of the economic scissors as a matter of percentages when we review the activities of a factory worker (an economic structure) who rents a home. In this case, all the resources have been reduced to money, and money is used for all outgoes. Moreover, the resources come to the person at regular times. Since the outgoes usually follow a monthly cycle and the incomes a weekly cycle, we will treat the income as being monthly to coincide with the outgoes. We will use an income of $2,000 a month in this example.

Before we can look further into this example, we know that taxes are paid before the worker receives his check. Other deductions are taken out as well. Health care and other benefits provided by an employer require deductions. Voluntary enrolments or the worker in programs that the employee considers most important also reduce the available resources to the take-home pay. Since $400 should cover this expense, take-home pay should be $1,600. This amount becomes 100 percent of his resources for subsequent considerations.

When he receives his check, the first priority for a factory worker is to pay rent. Housing experts tell us that payments for housing should not exceed 30 percent of gross income, so the worker must pay $600 for rent. At this point, his available resources are reduced from $1,600 to $1,000. Although the percentage of rent to gross resources is 30 percent, the percentage of rent to available resources is 37.5 percent.

Normally, groceries are next and become the first priority after rent. In a typical month, a normal family can exist on $400. To be nourished may require $600. For this example, we will use the higher figure. Six hundred dollars ($600) is 30 percent of the gross salary, but 60 percent of available resources (which are now $1,000) at this point in the worker's mind. His available resources have been reduced from $1,000 to $400.

Now another requirement becomes the first priority. A worker requires the ability to travel to work. If a bus is available, this expense is minimal, but usually he uses a car. An average cost for a car amounts to about $200 per month. Now, the percentages are 10 percent of the gross income, but 50 percent of the available resources. After this expense, he has $200 of available resources left.

The next possible use for the money might require $300 for a new lawn mower. This is only 5 percent of the gross salary, but is more than 100 percent of his available resources. Since he does not have available resources to continue, he is now out of the economy and cannot be considered when economists look at demand. In many cases, there are several possibilities for the use of the money. Some of these other uses require less than the remaining available resources. By changing the first priority to one of these uses, some other objective is accomplished. Another possibility is to hold the money until the following month and increase his available resources then by $200.

The factory worker is a simple example of the way economic demand is limited by resources. Even here, the picture can be complicated easily. By working overtime, the employee can increase his income. By owning his home free and clear, rent is not involved, although other housing costs may be added. If the individual is laid off and cannot work, the example ceases to be valid. Because every change in circumstance changes the situation of the economic structure, the idea that any person at any time can determine what any other individual can accomplish is laughable.

Since mathematical scissors apply to each economic structure, all outgoes are a percentage of the income of the structure. What the outgo is called is immaterial. Social Security paid by the employee of a company cannot be distinguished from Social Security paid by the company so far as outgo of the company is concerned. This reminds us that as either the absolute income amount or the absolute outgo price changes, the relationship of each outgo to all other outgoes also changes.

INTERACTION OF THE BLADES OF THE MATHEMATICAL SCISSORS

Sometimes the effort to deal with one blade of the scissors, such as outgo, without observing how it affects the other blade, such as income, causes people to make idiotic decisions, such as this one: A stepmother detested her stepson. On the death of his father, the stepson became the heir to a house with a life estate to the stepmother. She had a manager rent the house with an instruction that only emergency repairs would be made. She received $700 a month rent and felt that she was doing well. What she didn't understand was that the proper rent for the house was $1,200 a month, but her manager could not rent it for that price. He decided that the only people who would rent a house that was not maintained were those who would not be allowed to rent elsewhere. For the failure to pay around $3,000 dollars a year occasionally, she deprived herself of $6,000 a year regularly. It is not the amount paid that matters, but the difference between what is paid and what is received.

Or this: Two European companies had subsidiaries in the United States. When they merged, they decided that their American subsidiaries should be placed under one control. At the same time they purchased another subsidiary, International Salt, now Akzo-Nobel Salt. The CEO of American Enka, another subsidiary that produced rayon and nylon yarn, was placed in charge of all the subsidiaries. American Enka had about eight hundred customers who bought significant quantities of their product. International Salt had every municipality in the Snowbelt as customers, each buying a small quantity of salt. The new CEO felt that the salesmen for both companies should be paid equivalent amounts, even though the requirements for selling salt demanded far more work than the requirements for visiting a few yarn mills. Sales of salt plummeted immediately, and International Salt had its first loss ever. It was not what was paid that mattered, but the difference between what was paid and what was received.

Or this: A doctor left Alaska, where prices were very high, and relocated to North Carolina, where prices were very low. He sold his four-room cabin in Alaska for $125,000, and wanted to buy in North Carolina under tax rules, then current, that allowed him to avoid taxes if he invested more in his new home than he received from his old one. He informed his realtor that he had to have a house worth at least $125,000. His realtor realized that there were no houses in that area that were listed at that high a price, but he had a friend who was considering selling his home, and the friend was expecting about $80,000. The realtor suggested listing the home for $125,000. The doctor bought the house. The doctor paid $45,000 for the privilege of not paying $15,000 in taxes. It is not the amount paid that matters, but the difference between what is paid and what is received.

As more and more subeconomies are included in the mix, the requirements and the rule continue to control. Despite the fact that young mothers buy diapers and old men travel, the overall mix of goods and services in the economy tend to develop an overall stable structure. As more and more subeconomies are added to the mix, they tend to be subject to the laws of large numbers. When this happens, statistical inference becomes a realistic tool to enable observation of what is happening. Economic forecasts, statistical ratios, and other indicators become valuable tools to use in determining what decisions need to be made.

This applies only while the economy is relatively stable. However, most economies that are not on a war footing are comparatively stable; economic indicators are a major benefit to the economy. On the other hand, when these indicators are published, the values they study have already been acted upon and expired. They are reactive. To enable the economy to be stable in the future and to improve, proactive measures need to be used. This requirement parallels the difference between understanding values before exchanges and understanding prices afterward.

RESOURCES WITHOUT STABLE OUTGOES

Values before a transaction are based upon whether the acquisition can fulfill an objective or not. Without objectives, then the economy is like a train without rails. We continue to buy and spend, but without rational purpose for doing so and with no direction.

A fairly simple example is the situation of a teenager when he has a new job. The teenager has few objectives of his own. There is no need for his paying rent since a home is provided by his parents, along with food and most of his necessities. In such a situation, the ability to spend money without having a structure established, without having planned objectives, means that the teenager is not bound by any restrictions that apply to other individuals. In such a situation, a teenager must find his own objectives. The source of such objectives must lie in the environment in which he lives.

We talk of "role models." Sometimes the objectives that a teenager obtains are set by a wish to imitate a particular person. Among these possible examples are such people as action heroes. It is simple to follow his example. If you examine the action hero's image and skills, you know any jackass can do what he does. Our current attitude about what we expect of young people makes it easy for the youth to expect and receive approval of his peers for such actions—that is, following the lead of spurious role models.

Others choose examples from the people where they live. It is easier for a girl to copy her mother as she often has a chance to be with her, than for a boy to recognize someone who is a sound model. Sometimes boys are kept away from male role models by mothers who believe that "boys need to enjoy their childhood" or "all men are beasts." These mothers fail to realize that the man the boy becomes is no different from the boy they indulged or denigrated.

Sometimes the teen obtains his objective from being influenced by advertising. Some boys save money regularly to buy a car or some other advertised merchandise. Even though these objectives seem to be limited, attaining such an objective encourages development of a sound system of values. Regardless of the source of positive influences, such influences are in public interest economically.

WHEN THE OVERALL STRUCTURE IS UNBALANCED

There are percentages that apply to the economy as a whole that we must take into account. The whole economic structure is made up of individual economic structures. Young mothers need diapers for their children, while elderly women do not need baby diapers, but the overall percentage of young mothers and of elderly women tends to be stable in the population. The demand for diapers, then, becomes a more or less stable percentage of the total demand of the overall economic structure. Where the overall percentage of resources used reflects the overall requirements for goods and services, the economic structure will remain healthy. Where this is not the case, the imbalance of resources used for one purpose creates a hardship on those who are not part of that particular subeconomy.

For example, our society has a good health record. At any one time, only 1 or 2 percent of the population is incapacitated. Most of us are working or enjoying our lives. This percentage of need for health services compares to the 10–20 percent of our expenditures on health. This imbalance reduces the funds available for other parts of the economy.

Such an imbalance occurred at the turn of the twentieth century. By establishing a monopoly, the Standard Oil Companies, for example, could and did set the price of oil at a certain price; therefore, this company became a stable and somewhat secure place for people to invest. Since all the other forms of investment involved more risk, investors chose to place their money in that company, and money became scarce for other important businesses that needed funding to accomplish their objectives. Some adjustment became essential for people to continue to live, and the antitrust laws currently on the books were enacted. These laws did not completely solve the problem, but they succeeded enough in reducing the problem that the remaining difficulties could be ignored. Health care, drug, and judicial claims against the economy currently have risen to the point that similar actions need to be taken to ameliorate a similar problem.

All health services are monopolies by the nature of the service. Each person uses a particular doctor and health system. There is usually no shopping around, and second opinions are usually meant to confirm the validity of the first diagnosis rather than to secure a change of doctors. As Medicare and other plans have thrown money at the health system, the health system has found ways to catch it. The result is that the expenditures for health services are far in excess of the need for those services. In a later chapter, this book presents the idea of limiting profits in such monopolies to no more than the government interest rate. When you get to that part, remember health care.

SOME RESULTS OF THE MATHEMATICAL SCISSORS

One blade of the mathematical scissors is the recognizable price of a resource. That price is set by buyers, and the usual price is the lowest alternative price for the exact duplicate of that resource.

Yarn is a very competitive product. Some years ago, Saluda Yarns, a small manufacturer in Saluda, North Carolina, was in serious financial difficulty.

The accountant who was helping them noticed that the amount of the loss each year was the same amount as the Social Security tax payment. The basic cost of manufacturing yarn was the same for both Saluda Yarns and other producers, even when the production was in foreign countries. The additional cost required for Social Security could not be recovered because the price of the yarns they produced was determined by the price charged by companies located in other countries that did not have this expense. Competition in the marketplace causes many companies to be in this condition.

The effect of this condition occurs when extra costs are added that will not be recovered. Then an unfair situation arises. The extra costs will cause the less profitable business to fail. In the nineteenth century, bank notes from every bank in the country caused American business to constantly be sabotaged by people's inability to determine just how valuable money was when it was used away from the bank. Counterfeiting was rampant. Anyone with a printing press could print a note from a non-local bank, and only later would the recipient know he had lost his money. By the simple expedient of taxing the standard issuance of bank notes, banks were stopped from issuing confusing paper money, and government-printed money became the only legal tender. This additional cost was deliberate and had the desired effect. Extra costs caused banks to stop issuing notes. It is easy to see why extra costs will cause other businesses to fail as well.

When extra costs arise from the bad decisions of inept management, there is no reason to feel compassion for the failure of a company. If the extra costs arise by action of the government, however, the people have a right to feel cheated. A company that has the choice of moving to Juarez, Mexico, or El Paso, Texas, will pick Juarez if it has any business sense. The materials, labor, and all other costs will be the same. In Juarez, the company has only to pay the wages that correspond to take-home pay in El Paso. By moving across the Rio Grande, the business will save the cost of paying Social Security, an amount totalling about 13 percent. The resulting price may possibly be less than an El Paso company would pay in total costs.

Social Security has been one of the major causes of stability in the economy during the last fifty years, as we will discuss later. A customs tariff charge equal to the Social Security tax on imports would not create any real hardship on any importer, but would mean an immediate ability of the government to reduce those taxes on employees in both countries. By making domestic production viable, it might easily reverse the trade imbalance.

Another situation where government rules have had a real impact on the business scene in the United States has been the urbanization created by the minimum wage. Additional costs for transporting the product of a company means additional costs for placing the product on the market. Only those companies that are located near the market for their product can remain in business if transportation is a material cost. Depopulation of Nebraska is the direct result of the transportation costs for companies in that state. If minimum wage were reduced by 10 percent for companies at least fifty miles away from a major population center, the problems caused by urbanization could be somewhat alleviated.

Overall, the understanding of the nature of the mathematical scissors and the results that follow each action are essential to a pleasant and useful life.

CHAPTER SIX

I'd Rather Be (You Name It)

PRIORITIES

PSYCHOLOGISTS HAVE SAID that people value survival more than security, security more than belonging, belonging more than family, and family more than self-expression. Experience in various cultures says that this order may not be the right one, but does show that such a hierarchy exists. Availability of the resources required to fulfill these needs helps determine what that order is. You must look at what you think is most important in light of your own culture. Other cultures may be different.

Take this case: A contractor was hired by the Associated Reformed Presbyterian Church to build a hospital in Bulape, Democratic Republic of the Congo, once known as Zaire. He was surprised to learn that there is no word in the local language for food or house, and natives there must use French to discuss these ideas. Then he realized that a person has only to go out to a nearby tree and obtain food, and shelter is easily provided by certain placements of vegetation growing nearby. Moreover, a house has a tendency to invite other animals that would like shelter, such as snakes and mice. If food is stored, the hot humid climate encourages mold, mildew, rot, and rats. Not only are the usual needs for survival not the subject of any of these people's goals, but security is not of interest either. The normal value of savings and thrift does not exist in that climate. Their priorities are different from ours.

The first economic objective of people in Bulape is not survival and security, but appears to be belonging to a group. Status, language, and means of communication, such as dance, are prized rather than food or property. A similar situation applies in Brazil. Here the first priority involves preparation and participation in Carnival and the activities that culminate at that time. Tropical climates with plentiful vegetation tend to relate to this circumstance. The resources available to the people determine what is most important to them.

Emiliano Zapata was a principal participant in the Mexican Revolution of 1910. His interest (and the interest of his people) was limited to obtaining enough land to grow the crops that these people needed to live. Other participants in the revolution were interested in establishing a government and laws, but Zapata was only interested in what affected his people. This lack of interest in the things that mattered to the others caused the other revolutionary leaders to be so suspicious of his motives that he was assassinated.

(Remember our second digression, that issues of morality are no the subject of this book!)

In such a place, one of the surest ways of establishing a secure relationship with the dominant individual in the community is to sell oneself to that individual as a slave. The Brazilians rejected their emperor, Dom Pedro II, when he abolished this time-honored institution. Africa sold their slaves to each other—where there was a common understanding of roles of both master and slave—and then to the Europeans, who had no concept of the limitations of the system. This cross-cultural exchange has continued to this day, without either thoroughly understanding the roles and relationship that are appropriate in the "foreign" culture.

Psychologists in developed countries infer from the culture of which they are a part. Survival and security are the most important motivations to cause people to act. In other cultures where food and shelter are not a problem, people do not act to satisfy these needs. When another culture supplies those needs, even though they serve no economic purpose, the suppliers are encouraging activities that do not fit the needs of the recipients. In Africa, war occurs because the new influx of resources allows everyone to have status. Since status is only useful if it sets one off from another so that one can coordinate the activities of all, this becomes an intolerable situation. Status is easily obtained by everyone when this is the case, and because each can live without the other, coordination becomes impossible. The consequence is the destruction of any stable means for cooperation.

The result is war. Rwanda, Congo, Ivory Coast, Senegal, Sudan, and other African countries have suffered from this surplus of unneeded resources.

Earlier, our discussion of teenagers dealt with the idea that people can have too many resources in our culture as well.

It is not too difficult to realize that the infusion of money from oil in Nigeria and diamonds in Sierra Leone have made certain people wealthy. Others with less ability to grasp the wealth have first resented and then fought for what they have. There is little need for the money in viable economies that provide what normally comes from the efforts of the local people. In this position, the objective that can be fulfilled does not include food or material things. The battles that have resulted have been for status, not for any useful purpose.

Each individual economic structure determines what its first priority is. Many women spend time preparing meals and enjoy the time spent eating. When the meal is finished and they are complimented on it, they feel that their efforts have been warranted. Their first-priority needs have been fulfilled.

Their guests, however, may have attended the meal as a part of a conference. To them, the meal is only a pause preceding their first-priority activity. Even while the first customer is eating the meal, they may be conversing on their real first-priority activity by continuing the discussions of the conference. While relationships sometimes require concern about the first priority of others, unless it happens that the activities of all the parties coincide exactly, there is no time when two economic activities have the same priority.

PRIORITIES BY LEVELS

Although the ideas that will follow are important to every individual, the most identifiable examples are to be found in businesses. While we are discussing major businesses here, every person has to determine whether his priority is an immediate goal or whether it is a goal that supports some future purpose.

When BASF manufactures thread, its first priority is satisfying the objective of the weavers. When the weavers make cloth, their first priority is satisfying the objectives of shirt manufacturers. Shirt manufacturers try to satisfy the objectives of wholesalers, then retailers, and then the buyers.

This system of relationships between the individual economic entities illustrates that what is a first-priority objective of one business is a secondary, third, or greater priority of another. In the general economy, they all play a part to accomplish the first priority of satisfying the goals of the eventual user. That first priority (the objectives of the buyers) appears to be matched by the other six priorities, and equal effort is spent on each, but the effects of the overall economy on them differs from one to another. Anticipation of the requirements of the first priority users of goods and services becomes more and more difficult as the priorities get farther and farther away from the first priority status.

This distance from the end use means that when a change in the economic activity level occurs, the lower priorities become more and more at risk of being affected by that change. An economic slowdown (in the above example) can be expected to cause layoffs in the thread mill first. When your goal is to become a doctor, you studying your lessons that relates to a distant goal is more likely to be dropped if you are hungry or cold, and where relief, not information, is an immediate goal.

BASF, making thread, and weavers, wholesalers, retails, and consumers have first-priority objectives that require different goods and services to accomplish their goals. With this diverse list of goods and services, it would seem that there would not be a common economic environment. However, over time and a constant situation, the overall economy is very stable. Again, young mothers buy diapers, and older women take cruises. The continuing replenishment of goods and services that both consumers require averages out. They are part of a whole economic environment that is the sum of all the component economic structures.

Where demand (the combined valuation of a specific item) is a combination of the requirements of one part of the economic environment, we can determine it by adding up all those component parts and determining how much will be required. For instance, just so many diapers will be needed each week. We can set the manufacturing of diapers to produce that amount. In turn, the doctoral student will study the subjects that are needed for class now and not take on subjects that will arise later.

THE DIFFERENCE BETWEEN FIRST-PRIORITY
AND LOWER-PRIORITY OBJECTIVES

This discussion of what comes first is important because the first-level demand takes precedence over every other objective when the mathematical scissors comes into play. Every other economic value is set aside when the first priority objective must be met. As the absolute price of the first-priority objective rises to the point that total resources cannot meet the price, the individual is forced out of the economic mix of which he is a part. If the doctoral student cannot pay his tuition, he must delay his studies. Either he must abandon that objective or must rethink and strategize how to satisfy his first-priority need. If he does not abandon the objective, he will abandon the economy. He may rebel against it if he is unable to satisfy his objective.

At times in every society, starvation and drought may make resources so scarce that no amount of effort will obtain them. When this happens, either the people die or migrate. Mexican immigration to the United States can easily be explained by this process.

First-priority objectives often involve avoiding things that are feared. (Again we must remember our second digression. What we are discussing is not a moral issue, but an issue of reality). Alcohol, drugs, and tobacco (as well as food) are the most frequent and most sure of the commodities placed on the market. Initially, each has the ability to eliminate boredom. Later, the fear of the consequences of withdrawal from their use makes their value to the user greater than anything else. Alcohol was the basis of the rise of the Mafia during Prohibition. The British gained economic control of China during the opium wars by supplying opium to the Chinese. Tobacco provided the value that made Virginia able to survive. (Food, in most cultures, is the only sure need and has a similar demand situation, but there is no moral issue involved.)

It is said in military circles, the ability to tolerate boredom is the most important attribute of a good soldier. The same problem occurs with firemen who must spend more time waiting for a fire than fighting it. People think of the military as exciting and full of activity, but the majority of a soldier's life is spent in waiting for something to happen, and a fireman works only when there is a fire. Man is not intended to sit still.

The officer who does not provide some activity during the wait will find his charges doing something just to "kill time." Avoiding boredom then is the first objective of most humans. If it cannot be avoided, substitutes such as alcohol or drugs become attractive. Then the use of overstimulants (alcohol, drugs, tobacco) becomes a problem. Once overstimulants take effect, their characteristic as a first-priority objective makes them so important to the user that everything else becomes valueless. Efforts to eliminate these problems must provide relief from both the fear of withdrawal and relief from boredom before any possible solution will work.

First-priority objectives are important because no activity occurs with any other priority. Even though the goal may be a second priority to another company, it must be a first priority to the person or business before they act. As a first-priority objective is attained or abandoned, some secondary or tertiary objective replaces it and becomes a first-priority objective. A person compares his resources with his ability to attain his first-priority objective and decides that there are enough resources or that there are not enough resources to accomplish that aim. Once that decision is made and acted upon, the first priority objective is satisfied, and another objective rises to the level of first priority. Economic activity is a succession of transactions, each satisfying some first-priority objective. Every economic transaction is an individual action. The appearance of multiple transactions comes from the quantity of transactions and the common practice of waiting to complete a separate transaction until others can be done at the same time.

Second-priority objectives are plans that are waiting in the wings or are necessary to the accomplishment of first-priority aims. Priorities beyond that are successively less important to economic activity, but as resources are perceived to be increased, they are advanced toward the status of first priorities. A tax cut to encourage spending can be considered a means of increasing the priority of second- or lower-priority objectives by making them more nearly possible to accomplish.

BUSINESS, LIVING, AND COORDINATION

If a company has a business of wrecking houses, it will wreck as many houses as it is paid to wreck. A business that builds houses will build as many houses as it is paid to build. But the two companies cannot be working at the same site at the same time. Either you are building or wrecking, but not both. The same rule applies as first-priority objectives are determined. Many people attempt to accomplish many objectives at the same time. The result is chaos in their economic structure. Eventually, when resources have been scattered over too many objectives, we find that few are accomplished. This leads to impoverishment of people, even when there are many resources.

This rule applies in an individual life, and it carries through to our community lives. One of the most critical objectives of any person, business, or other entity is to obtain cooperation with other entities so that their activities are not at cross-purposes at the same place and during the same time. The most elementary form of obtaining this coordination is to fight it out, and the winner of a fight determines what is to be done. Historically, this is the standard method of resolving differences. It is also the least efficient method.

Coordination, as we discovered earlier, involves making allowances for the satisfaction of all objectives that are needed. When the winner of a fight coordinates activities, the objectives that are meaningful to him are satisfied, but there is no way for him to know all the objectives that are important to everyone. As a result, many important functions of society are overlooked. Such a situation occurred during the life of the Soviet Union. A farmer might need fertilizer, but approval for obtaining it meant that he needed to go through channels that might have reached as far as the Kremlin. Those in the appropriate bureau in Moscow had no real idea of what was happening in the field. What the farmer needed then was not available at the right time and in the right quantities.

The same circumstance applies now to medical insurance in the States. Insurance companies require that they approve doctor's treatments according to their rules. To satisfy those rules requires so much time that treatment time is reduced. When patient time is reduced, each patient must pay more to provide the same income to the doctor. Such a situation automatically increases medical costs, with no such increase in service.

The priority of any objective, including coordination, is a major factor in apportioning resources, both in our individual lives and in our communities.

CHAPTER SEVEN

Budget Your Goals, Not Your Silver

SETTING PRIORITIES

SETTING PRIORITIES IN your goals is a type of budgeting. Value relates to the ability of something to accomplish or assist in accomplishing some goal. We have shown that every person has an economic structure that consists of a set of resources and needs. Resources are what is available to be used to accomplish objectives, and needs are the things that are required to accomplish a person's or an organization's objectives. It follows that objectives are the most important element in economics.

If we budget our money, we have only accomplished part of what we need to be effective in our economic life. To be effective, we need to budget our objectives first, which allows us to budget our money. When you budget each of your goals first, the silver will fall in line.

To say that we have no objectives would be silly. We must eat, sleep, and avoid boredom if we do nothing else. If you think you haven't any objectives to accomplish, we suggest that you take a closer look at how you're living and obtain some. When we have many resources and no objectives to be accomplished, we find ourselves wasting all we have. The unhappy endings to stories of lottery winners who live penniless is because they have spent or lost all their winnings—a result of a failure to determine what goals their winnings should have been used for.

It is important to determine what your goals are. Once you have determined what you want to do, the money you have can be allocated to accomplishing what you want to accomplish.

STABILITY

You are an economic entity. As such, you have an economic structure that consists of resources and needs that either have become or will become stable. You use your resources either to accomplish your goals, exchange for money or other resources, or waste.

You have goals that you want to accomplish; that is to say, needs that you want to fulfill. These terms are synonymous. These needs include eating, sleeping, acceptance by your friends, mating, avoiding boredom, or any other goals you have chosen and found that you have the resources to do.

These goals will change over time, but you will resist such change until you understand that the new goals will enhance or strengthen your economic structure. For the present, you have a consistently stable economic structure. For the factory worker, that structure will be to go to work, receive a paycheck, shop in certain stores for groceries. If there is enough in the paycheck, the structure will include a favorite hobby, entertainment, or use for the family. You will watch television for subjects that you can talk over with your friends, and you will do this each day as long as you find that there are no essential goals overlooked.

For the salesman, you will organize your time, make friends with customers, and watch the amount of cash that is available until the next sale. Your goals will include many of those goals that the factory worker has, but you will not necessarily approach and achieve them in the same ways. Every individual has an economic structure that he has developed over time.

You are part of larger economic entities. These larger economic structures include your family, your business or workplace, your church or social organization, your community, your political subdivision, your political group, and eventually the nation and the world. For you, these entities or structures serve a purpose. In turn, they have goals that they want to accomplish. When these goals agree with your own, the coordination of your efforts with others will enhance your ability to accomplish both your own and the organization's aims. When there is disagreement over goals and people who work against each other, nothing will be accomplished.

You want these organizations to be stable as well, and you need to understand how they affect your life, but first you need to understand your own personal economic structure.

RECOGNIZE YOUR OBJECTIVES

When Will Rogers laughed and said, "The Baptists and the bootleggers will vote dry as long as they can stagger to the polls," everyone laughed with him. There was little concern that there was a reason that they voted for prohibition as they did. They laughed because it really happened and was in contradiction of their avowed purposes. In a dry state, the bootleggers could easily get rid of competition and increase the value of their product by continuing to officially maintain the Prohibition laws.

The Baptist's purpose was subtler. They did not believe in the word or idea of a "creed." Without a clear understanding of what they believe in common, usually called a creed, they would not have had a common purpose to keep them together. Their covenant that replaced the creed in their theology included a paragraph about refraining from all liquors, and prohibition was a means by which they could demonstrate their adherence to that covenant. People may not understand all the reasons they act as they do, but they are not stupid. Every action has a reason that relates to some objective.

People sometimes go to the grocery store hungry. When they see something that will satisfy their hunger, they buy it, but they don't eat it immediately. They have not satisfied their hunger, so the next thing that will satisfy their hunger looks good to them. They buy that also, but still, since they didn't eat it, it doesn't satisfy their hunger. As this continues, they end up buying far more than they can use. Later they ask themselves, "Why did I buy that?" They have not recognized that their goal was to satisfy their hunger, and by attempting to accomplish this goal without fulfilling it, they have overbought. The saving is, "Don't go to the grocery store hungry. Eat first." By eating first, you have eliminated hunger as a factor in deciding what to buy. You have recognized your objective.

Recognizing your goals entails understanding yourself. We often make the mistake of having feelings that we consider "wrong" or "evil." We choose to be someone that is not "us." For example, to take the goal of losing weight too seriously is to become anorexic. Despite the fact that there is no more weight available to lose, you continue to diet, and major health problem ensues. The problem is that we take some "authority" as our guide and attempt to please it in our minds. Whatever we are, we are. We are not created to be something that we decide is better than we are, but as we are. We can change if it can be shown what the change is as it affects us ourselves, but to accept anyone else's opinion of what we should be is to court disaster. No person should criticize himself for what he is. Whatever he is, is acceptable.

When we recognize that we are whatever we are, we learn to deal with it in a rational way. Take this case: A soldier was on KP duty one day, and an assistant cook decided to ride him. During eight solid hours, for everything he did, this cook told him it was wrong. Finally, with a knife in reach, the soldier moved to stab the cook. As he did so, the chief cook said for everyone to go to the barracks, and the stabbing didn't happen. The soldier could have said that he was not a murderer since no one was killed. Instead he said, "In conditions like that, of being senselessly harassed, I could murder someone. I am a murderer." Because he accepted that he might respond the same way in future situations, he has avoided those situations, knows how to keep his impulses under control, and will never murder anyone.

When we don't recognize who we are, we find ourselves looking very foolish. A man invited a coworker home one night. There was a gallon of wine available, and the guest, within a short time, drank most of it, all the time saying, "I can handle my liquor. I'm not an alcoholic." This man could not hold a job and was frequently in need, yet he could not understand why people thought he was not reliable. In this case, his objective was to become drunk, and he wouldn't accept that that was his aim.

EVALUATE YOUR OBJECTIVES

There was a family who overvalued education. There was a daughter in that family who excelled in athletics and was a typical teenager, a junior in high school. She cut school one day. To her mother, this was a serious crime, and the mother reacted accordingly. The punishment was severe and humiliating in front of the daughter's peers. In fact, it was so humiliating that the daughter didn't want to face her schoolmates for her senior year, but no one in her family was willing to accept that fact. The only way the daughter could see to avoid the humiliation of facing her class for another year was to become pregnant, and she did. At no time did she entertain the thought of being a housewife, but the boy chose to marry her, and the family acquiesced. The girl ignored her husband and chose to continue acting like a daughter in her old family. Finally, when her husband realized what was going on, he divorced her.

Here we have a case of failing to properly evaluate the goals involved. Education is only one part of life. The mother's insistence on education, even to punishing when there was only a normal teenage response, is an example of overreaction. When the mother insisted that the daughter be perfect, the punishment involved was not in any way related to the crime. When the predictable response of the daughter, wanting to avoid further embarrassment, was frustrated, that too was overreaction. The daughter's goal of avoiding her peers was not as valuable as learning to be a wife and mother, and the husband's goal of a family of his own was unrealistic. To place too much value on any goal finds us willing to destroy other goals that are just as valuable. There are many other examples like this that we see in families all the time.

ACCEPT THE PAST, ANALYZE THE PRESENT, DEAL WITH THE FUTURE

There was a doctor who loved to hug his patients. One of these patients was mentally deficient. One day he hugged her, and the girl told everyone that he had "loved" her. Her parents misunderstood what had happened, took the case to court, and the doctor was convicted of a sexual assault. He was required to sell his practice and live as a guest of the tax-payers for a number of years.

Had the parents chosen to verify the nature of the medical evidence, take the daughter to another doctor in the future, and simply avoided the doctor, there would have been no expense for prison upkeep, a doctor would have been available in the town, court costs would have been saved, and a doctor's good reputation would have been saved. Instead, the family wanted "revenge."

Revenge is the result of a wish to change the past. What's done is done and cannot be undone. The efforts to "right wrongs" and atone for the past are always a waste. This applies in every case, yet we feel that we must strike back whenever we are hurt. Obviously, if someone can be expected to cause the same hurt in the future, the situation is different. Then prompt, adequate, and effective action must be taken. But why would one hold a grudge against someone when it is easier to eliminate the problem? One needs, for his own sake, to accept the past, analyze the present, and deal with the future.

An excellent example of this is found in the parable of the prodigal son. At some point, he "came to himself." This infers that he analyzed his situation: "Even the servants in my father's house are treated better than this." He then decided what he would do. "I will arise and go to my father." He further said that he would suggest that he was willing to be a servant. Then he acted on his decision. The parable is clear that he could not be restored to his heritage—that had been spent—and it infers that he became a servant since that was the only opening available. He had analyzed the situation, accepted the past, and planned for the future based on his possibilities.

Too many people expect the past to provide for the future. A woman who had spent her life away from home and only incidentally maintained a family relationship found that her father left nothing for her in his will. She spent her remaining assets trying to get her sister to give her a part of the estate. Recognizing that there was nothing there for her would have been painful, but would have allowed her to look at other prospects and make the best of what she had. In this case, she did not accept the past, which could not be changed, did not analyze her present to understand that what she was doing was not profitable, and her future was short, for she died soon after.

A word for this process is forgiveness. Too often, people assume that forgiveness involves restoration, but the parable of the prodigal son makes it clear that the son was not restored to his wealth that had been spent. The idea that restoration is inherent in forgiveness creates a problem. A son stole from his father, destroyed his father's property, told tales to the neighbors that ruined the father's reputation, and couldn't understand it when the father made sure his son was no longer involved in anything he did. The father had forgiven his son, but he could only expect that his son would repeat his past actions. The consequences of the past do not go away just because of forgiveness.

But the one most in need of forgiveness is not the other fellow. It is essential that when you are not perfect, you forgive yourself. No one else can know all that you feel you have done wrong as well as you do, and only when you accept the past, realizing that it will not be changed, can you look forward to what comes next.

SIMPLIFY YOUR OBJECTIVES

Women often choose to go shopping as a goal in itself. They spend time doing it and enjoy the process. A man will enter a store, go to the department, select a shirt, pay for it, and leave. To a man, the goal is to satisfy the need for a shirt and not to spend time in a store. He will simplify the process in order to spend (waste) less time on something that is not important to him. He will use that time to satisfy another goal. The difference here is that the woman has an important goal in shopping and will use her resources first in that endeavor. The man will spend little time as possible on a necessary goal that is not important to him. Whenever you have a necessary goal that is not important, a person should simplify the necessary to accomplish the important.

There is a saying, "If you're up to your waist in alligators, it's hard to remember that you are have come to drain the swamp." Our necessary goals are like alligators; they are in the way, make difficulties, and keep us from attempting to accomplish what is important. By hanging on to necessary goals, when they can be solved soon and easily, we retain our alligators. When Alexander the Great solved the riddle of the Gordian Knot by cutting it with the knife, he chose to ignore the difficulties that had stopped all the earlier attempts and deal with the problem directly. (The complicated knot had been tied and then connected to a prophecy that whoever untied it would rule Asia. Alexander had his objective well in mind.) It is possible that any person can find an easier way to accomplish the goals that they choose.

There is another way we can simplify our goals. Not every goal is either necessary or important. By analyzing goals, some will come up unnecessary. To these we should respond with the word no, whether the choice is ours or someone else's. "Nobody's got to do nothing," was the advice one uncle gave when the boy said he had to do something. Once this idea is accepted, you will find this advice valuable when people demand that you do what they want done.

This attitude has one real drawback. You do not have to do anything, but you do have to accept the consequences. Calling the fire department if your house is on fire is a part of the goal of saving your house. If you fail to call the fire department when your house is on fire, you are acting within your rights. It's your house. But do not expect to sleep in the house that night, or even sometime in the future. Always consider the consequences of your action or inaction. By anticipating what the results will be, you can choose to do what is best voluntarily. The coercion implicit in the words "You have to do this" may make you want to resist, but if you know the consequences and have the freedom to them, you will find the resentment involved gone.

ELIMINATE OBJECTIVES

Sometimes we feel that there are many, many objectives we want to accomplish, and we try to fulfill all of them. With a limit of resources available to us, the amount of resources we apply to each of them is inadequate. As a result, all of them suffer, and none of the objectives is accomplished. We usually accumulate objectives when we listen to others and allow them to decide what is important for us.

During the English Civil War, a certain cavalier was noted for his ability to squander his time and energy on many things. The people said that he "would get on his horse and ride off in all directions." By scattering his objectives, he lost the ability to accomplish any one of them. This saying has been part of the English idiom ever since. I have been told of many men who, like this, spoke big, got in other people's way when they were working on a goal, and drove in all directions, and did nothing.

CARRY THROUGH WITH OBJECTIVES

Once someone knows what his objective is, it is important to concentrate as much interest as possible on accomplishing that objective and persist. The late entertainer, pianist/comedian Victor Borge, told the story of his hapless uncle in many of his concerts. This uncle invented 1Up, 2Up, 3Up, 4Up, 5Up, and 6Up, but gave up before 7Up. It's not an uncommon story—having a good idea, but giving up on it too soon. A certain young man consistently developed prototypes of inventions that others later developed into profitable businesses. Due to the ridicule of his family, however, he gave up whenever problems arose. If problems stop a person from completing a job, he has only himself to blame. One must commit to accomplishing objectives, solve his problems, and go on.

RECOGNIZE LIMITATIONS AND ABILITIES

To try to accomplish a goal that is beyond one's ability without asking for help, however, is to make you look foolish. Typically, this happens when people listen to commercials that suggest a profitable objective, buy the product, and assume they can fit the objective into their timeframes. When this is clearly impossible, the purchase is a waste.

The ability to recognize what you can do and what you can't do is the most valuable ability that anyone can have. Many people waste more time trying to accomplish things that they are not suited for than time spent on what they are good at. Good brick masons spend their time learning and practicing the art of consistently placing the brick in exactly the right place. Such people typically are not trained in theology or any other study. Accountants make lousy salesmen, yet they wonder why people don't buy from them. When Jesus said, "If your eye be single, all your body will be full of light," he was referring to this concept. If you accept your limitations and enhance your abilities where it counts, you will be a reliable, contributing part of your society.

When you concentrate on your strength, you become stronger. When you ignore your limitations, it takes away from your strengths.

GET GOALS

There are employees who are constantly busy, finding things to do and working for their bosses even when the boss isn't around. Typically these employees remain on the job as long as they want to. There are others who need to be told what to do, slack off when the boss isn't around, and pass the time being bored. These employees typically last only a short time before they are laid off or fired. A sign in one business said, "You should be fired with enthusiasm, to avoid being fired with enthusiasm." Boredom is the result of not having an objective that you want to accomplish. If you don't have an objective, find one.

There are short-term and long-term goals. The long-term goal does require that you spend all your time on it. Wherever you are, there are thing that can be done. To allow boredom to begin is to place yourself at risk. Two women applied for clerical positions at the Forest Service office. Both were hired. The well-trained, intelligent applicant lasted only a short time. The untrained, average applicant remained for years. One boss said that the first applicant wasn't "hungry enough." Unless you are "hungry" enough to find a challenge in any situation, you will find yourself lost.

COORDINATE YOUR GOALS

If a builder and a wrecker try to work on the same house at the same time, one or the other will not accomplish anything. In your own life, you can fail to recognize that objectives cancel each other out. More critically, as you enter other combinations of economic entities that have economic structures, you could choose from among those ones having different aims than you do. You should avoid this. If your personal goals do not correspond to those of the organization of which you are a part, you have chosen to make yourself frustrated.

Most notorious of these combinations is marriage. If you marry for sex and find that your spouse wants no sex, you will soon ask for an annulment. More importantly, if you marry and find that your spouse dislikes the things you adore, wants to accomplish what you think is wrong, or cannot support what you want accomplish, you have chosen a course that will make your life impossible. It takes a determined and knowledgeable view of life to overcome such difficulties before they begin.

ACCEPT HELP

We are part of the world, and we need to interact with it. Many times we find that helping others to accomplish their goals becomes a goal in itself. Many other times, asking others to help you accomplish some goal provides a goal for them. By coordinating our actions with others and assisting them, we develop resources that make many more goals possible.

NEGATIVE GOALS, POSITIVE GOALS

If you buy ten new stocks as they come on the market, you may lose the value of nine of them. You would think that you have lost everything. But the tenth one could be another Microsoft. That stock increased in value since its appearance on the market so much that the loss from the other nine stocks means nothing. Some people try to be secure and never suffer loss. These people will never have more than what they started with. They have a negative view of life. Such a view automatically dooms the person to a life of protecting what they have.

The ultimate security is to know that so many years from now (never more than a hundred), they will not be alive, and they will have nothing. Knowing this, they enter into each activity with gusto and live during the years that they have. These people have a positive view of life and enjoy it.

The Bible has a saying for this: "He who would save his life will lose it, He who would lose his life for my sake will save it" (Matt. 16:25). This adds a new caveat to the idea of positive thinking. If you use your life to contribute to your world, you will not suffer. The idea could be understood as saying that you can do whatever you want to do because you will die anyway. Such an interpretation does not bring happiness. It is contributing to the world of which you are a part that is rewarding. Positive thinking involves doing those things that make life better and allows the possibility that life will include much more because of your attitude.

Negative thinking limits your income to what you have now. Positive thinking increases that income and removes limitations.

Once you have budgeted your objectives, budgeting your money will follow naturally. More importantly, a budget based on realistic objectives will be effective.

ENJOY THE RESULTS

Nothing makes life more enjoyable than the knowledge that you have accomplished some goal, no matter how small. Celebrate, have a party, and let everyone know that you are enjoying the results of your efforts. Birthdays, anniversaries, new jobs, projects completed—anything that you can have done and done well needs to be something that you are proud of. Celebrate.

PART THREE

YOU AND EVERYONE ELSE

CHAPTER EIGHT

Economic Structures

LET'S REVIEW

WE HAVE MENTIONED economic structures several times in this book and how an individual's economic structure is the basis for the economic structure of the whole economy. That is, each individual is in his or her place an important part of the world's economy. We need to accept that importance and understand that the world would be a different place if any one of us did not exist. You are a basic economic structure.

Since economic structures are so important, it's impossible to go on without a review.

THE NATURE OF COMPLEX STRUCTURES

We turn now to the ways that individuals, as less complicated structures, relate to the overall economy, which is really complex.

Complex economic structures have many different forms and organizations. For example:

- Al and Bill became partners in a partnership, Albill, Inc. Al owed thousands of dollars, while Bill had a great deal of money in the bank. Albill, Inc. lasted only a short time because its economic structure could not reconcile the differences in attitude between Al and Bill.

- Dave and Ellen got married in a union we will call forever. Dave wanted to invest and have funds available for future use, while Ellen never had the need for saving money and spent without caring where it was going. The couple developed such friction that the marriage, forever, fell apart.
- A child was born to a Mende couple in Africa. Its resources were its parents caring for it, and its needs included food, shelter, and a community of caring adults. The child thrived.

Each of these descriptions deals with several economic structures. There are, however, some common elements in all economic structures. They contain and are involved in obtaining resources, attaining goals, and are organized around a set of ideas of the nature of reality. Moreover, they involve actions on the part of the participants.

Complex economic structures are economic structures that involve two or more people. The first rule of all economic structure is this: If the outgo the structure exceeds the income, the upkeep becomes its downfall. No matter how simple or complex the structure is, this rule applies. But the rule embraces the additional understanding that income is dependent upon resources. In turn, resources are dependent on contributions, and contributions are, in turn, dependent on the willingness of others to value what is contributed toward goals they determine they want to accomplish.

Whew, what a sentence! Let's simplify: Income is dependent on objectives. This chain of dependencies is the real essence of economics. Every part of it depends on the determination that someone wants to accomplish some goal.

Each economic structure, beginning with the individual, has a hierarchy of things that it will use its resources for. Each structure is different. Old people do not buy baby diapers, and young people normally have no need for walking canes. It would seem that the combination of economic structures would require that individuals have a similar set of needs. The overall structure, however, can be stable even when individual needs are different. The combination of individuals in a marriage, for instance, would indicate a need for both shaving cream and lipstick. Neither spouse uses both, but together the married couple has requirements that is as stable as if each of the pair needed both. In the marriage, the same rule applies. If the outgo exceeds the income, the upkeep becomes the downfall.

As more and more subeconomies are included in the mix, the requirements laid down by this rule continue to control.

ECONOMIC STRUCTURES AS ORGANISMS

To restate a few important points: Economic structure (of which you are one) is the real basis of economics. Every transaction involves at least one structure, and every transaction depends on the nature of the economic structure, or structures, involved. Most economists are interested in the transaction since the transaction is a measurable quantity. A price has been set. The values that exist before that transaction occurs (the values you set) determine whether a transaction occurs or not. These values are a function of the economic structures involved. Study of the transactions that ensue is dependent on the nature of the structure.

In a previous chapter, we read that economic activity is similar to an organism, such as the human body. In the human body, the blood, nerves, and hormones act as connecting points between the individual cells and the rest of the body. Given that money has a benchmark quality that is recognized both by the individual and the rest of society, money serves a function similar to blood in the economic structure. Information compares to nerves, and relationships compare loosely with hormones.

An economy exists in a particular environment. All economies have many parts, which may be economies as well. They flourish if there are resources to nourish them and produce waste, which must be disposed of. Economies are stable with definable limits. An economy recruits new business to replace failures. Books and other mechanisms, like nerves, define the activities of economies and allow for correction of inefficient activities. The nature of an economy can enable people to recognize it as an economy and differentiate from all other economies. All the requirements that apply to any organism are present in economies. To study economies as if they were organisms is appropriate and to be desired.

INTERDEPENDENCY—PANACEAS

In dealing with the expansion of economic thinking from the individual to the community, we need to look at how everything fits together.

It is said of economists that they have to explain everything before they can explain anything. This is a truth that makes little sense to the average individual, but is true nonetheless. Every economy has an organic structure that can never be stopped for study. It would not work if it stood still. Even if only a part of it were not working, it would not be fully effective. Doctors have to work with the body the same way. During an operation, every function of the body must be maintained. So it is with economics. Even when we isolate a function of economics, it may have different effects on different parts of the economy while it is being described.

One of the hardest concepts to understand is the idea that panaceas do not work. We are told one idea or another will be the cure-all and solve the problems of the world, and we implement the idea without observing the consequences. Famine relief in Somalia was to be relieved with food but destroyed the Somali economy. Wells in the Sahel, between the Sahara Desert and the African rain forests, were supposed to help the cattle grazers. Because the grazing near the wells was soon eaten up, the herders had to choose between water for their cattle and food for their cattle.

The panacea, well, made the situation worse rather than better.

Economic activity is an interdependent activity. Panaceas do not work.

THE INTANGIBLE ECONOMY

Unlike the body, the economic structure is not physically identifiable, but does tend to locate in a specific area. Boundaries of economic areas of influence are not clear. People who are culturally part of southern regional influences are to be found in Ohio, while a manufacturing mentality typical of more northern influence can be found in West Virginia. Even within economic areas, various cultural backgrounds apply to different economic structures. The most glaring are such cultural divergences as those arising from migratory origins. People arriving from a Northern European location require that food must be saved and stored for winter use. Failure to do this is a sign of sloth and worthlessness. People from an equatorial location know that storage of food brings vermin and rot. To them, storage of food means there is a person among them who is likely causing disease and problems. Where these different cultures exist together, mutual antagonisms involved must be resolved or ignored. To demand adherence of one by the other is foolishness.

When economies are viewed as organisms rather than discipline, some interesting results develop. For example, an economy may be found to exist without any money involved, as in some village cultures of West Africa.

On the shores of Lake Victoria in Africa, there are tribes who exist on fish taken from the lake. There are other tribes who live alongside them who exist on cattle and cattle products. These tribes have separate economies. In western Africa, the Mende are agriculturalists, while the Fulani base their economy on cattle. The Mende welcome the Fulani when they travel across their land because the manure fertilizes their crops. These are separate economies, but they have a symbiotic relationship.

Farmers in America typically operate separately, but cooperate in marketing and cooperative buying. Each is separate, but exists in a cooperative economic structure. A corporation, on the other hand, is a full-fledged economy of its own. Here the subeconomies are coordinated to act in an efficient manner.

ORGANISMS AND NUTRITION

A physical body ingests food, processes it, distributes it to the places that need it, uses it, and disposes of it. This is true of economic organisms as well. A cotton seed is useless by itself. Unless it is put in the ground to grow or crushed for meal or oil, there is no value in it. When it is put in the ground to grow, there is a possibility of future value, but only as time develops it. When it is grown and cotton bolls produce the fiber, there are competing needs that provide more value, but its real value is still in the future. Part of the cotton is woven into, for example, shirts, and at this point there is potential value. If a shirt reaches the hands of a person who can wear it, the value is finally made evident, since value derives from the usefulness of the item. Until the product becomes useful, only potential value exists.

Value deteriorates. Use of the shirt causes wear and tear, and eventually the shirt becomes useless again. At that time, there is value in disposing of the worn shirt. The replacement of the shirt follows the same course, from usefulness to value and back to uselessness. The product cycle is a linear cycle that has a beginning and an end. It appears to be continuous because each shirt when disposed of is replaced by another. However, for the individual shirt, the value cycle goes from beginning to end, from worthless, to valuable, to worthless again.

The organism continues, however. Blood is a distribution system that takes the products of digestion to the place where it is needed in the body continuously moves through the body and disposes of the waste. Money is similar to blood in the economic cycle. Economists frequently talk about the monetary cycle. I pay you, you use the money to pay someone else, and after many transactions, some of the money you have spent comes back to me. This continuous financial cycle is similar to blood circulation in the body. Like blood, it is most useful when it continues to flow. When blood stops, it congeals, and the constrictions that occur because of the stoppage become life-threatening. When monopolies acquire all the money that is needed by the whole economy, the lack of funding available for other necessary functions destroys the economy. Monopoly is the subject of another chapter.

There are many points where the linear production cycle touches the circular money cycle. When money is put into a product, that money becomes an investment. When the product is put in use, there is an expectation that it will be more valuable to the purchaser than all the investment.

This expectation is what makes people invest in future value. Each time an investment is made, there is an interaction between the two cycles.

WHEN RESOURCES EXCEED EXPENDITURES: AN EXAMPLE

Economic structures arise fortuitously, but are stable and continuous so long as resources exceed expenditures as a whole within the total structure. An example of how this can occur is inferred in one hypothesis of the rise and fall of the Viking Empire.

We need to set the stage first. Earlier we quoted from two sections of A History of Rome by Moses Hadas. The first quote described how farmers were unable to farm because they owed so much money to Romans. Since the concept of bankruptcy hadn't been invented at that time, there was no ready relief for this problem. The second described how the people no longer claimed to be Romans. St. Remigius was a bishop of Rheims during this period and realized two things: debts needed to be cleared, and an effective government needed to be established. He accomplished the second task by accepting the Franks as the rulers in what was then Gaul, choosing them over the Visigoths, Lombards, and Vandals, who failed to believe in the essence of the church's teachings.

Remigius solved the first problem by promoting a variant interpretation of the Bible. By saying that interest (usury in the definitions of the time) was a sin, he gave people a reason to refuse to pay their debts to the Romans. This solved the immediate problem, but destroyed the ability of the people to invest their money in improving their condition. Without interest, loans were not forthcoming, and business died. The Middle Ages in Europe floundered in this inhospitable business climate.

People still amassed money as they went about their business, but without a means to invest for a purpose, they looked for a way to use it. The church taught that you should "lay up for yourselves treasures in heaven." The church itself was as near heaven as a man could be then, so wealth was placed in the church. Churches were meant to be accessible, so they were built close to where people lived and could easily reach.

A story comes to mind: Perhaps a fisherman from Norway was blown to England by a storm. While the storm abated, he sought shelter in the only place he could find, the church. Everyone else was home in bed, and there were many beautiful things lying around, so when he left, he took a few of these items with him. Arriving at home, he described the church and showed what he had taken. Since the pickings were so easy, other fishermen made the trip. Soon, a trip to loot the churches was a lark. The early descriptions of the actions of the Vikings show that if anyone stopped them in one place, they didn't fight but went to another. There were plenty of churches available that didn't have any defenses.

At home, the fishermen found that they could trade these finds to people farther east. Another trade had developed in that direction. Furs from Russia made good warm clothing, and Byzantine traders had established connections with Novgorod the Great, a city in northern Russia, where they bought the furs. There the Norsemen and Byzantines met, and silver and gold from English churches could be traded for Indian spices (brought overland to Trebizond or through northern Turkey to Egypt), military armor, and other things needed by the fishermen. Soon fishing was a part-time trade, and looting the churches came first. The armor and the military tactics learned while the Vikings spent time in Constantinople made them more able to force their will on the people who were providing their wealth. Eventually, they could not be stopped.

The Viking Empire extended from Western Europe through Visby, Novgorod, and Kiev to Constantinople. Different parts of this empire included mercenaries in the Byzantine army, fur trappers in Russia, traders in Visby, and sailors in Norway. A castle built on the Kattegat on the North Sea charged tolls on passing ships in the same manner as the city of Troy did at the time the Iliad was written. This enterprise indicated a very cohesive economic structure that was able to last. Several centuries later, the Mongols destroyed Kiev, isolated the northern part of the empire, and severed the trade routes.

Cut off from their markets in the east and out of loot to trade in the west, the Vikings raided England to obtain land to farm. Since the Vikings did not have a very strict government, and since every Viking benefited from supporting the others in their economic structure of looting, they were not used to governing. After they obtained all the land they needed for themselves, they allowed Alfred the Great to extend his government over them and became ruled by him in what is historically known as the Danelaw.

That they did not expect or want to be bothered by the government is illustrated by the efforts of William the Conqueror. He needed the "Harrying of North" (an armed foray into Northern England that killed many residents there) soon after the Conquest to subdue them. He had little problem extending his rule over the Anglo-Saxon areas of England, but was not accepted in the Danelaw until he destroyed many of the local institutions through a series of vicious raids that killed many of these inhabitants.

DYING ECONOMIES

We have just seen an example of a successful trading empire. But what happens when resources are no longer available?

In 1972, Colin Turnbull published a book called The Mountain People about a tribe in Africa that survived on hunting called the Ik. The Turkana and Dodo tribes that lived in the same area were flourishing, but the Ik were deprived of their hunting lands by establishment of Kidepo National Park. Their territory in Kenya had extended into Uganda and Sudan previously, but police in those countries had forbidden them entry to that part of their former territory. These restrictions on their use of the land deprived them of their former economic base, and Turnbull's book describes the destruction of relationships that developed because of these deficiencies.

The principle hypothesis of the book was that cooperation between individuals within the tribe ceased to exist, and individual selfish interests were the only interests left. Mothers abandoned their children whenever the children became a burden. The only way children were born was by rape, and theft was both expected and acceptable. Individuals separated themselves from others and only cooperated if they were able to gain something from the activity.

Whenever individuals perceive that hope for a better situation becomes impossible, the economic structure of which they are a part becomes superfluous. An example of this can be seen in Palestine today. Palestinian youths find it easier to commit suicide, taking others with them, than to continue to exist where there is no work, no chance for advancement, and no future.

This attitude is expressed in religious terms, but religion in this case is a smoke screen for hopelessness. People do not like to face the fact that their efforts are deemed to be worthless and rationalize events and situations in acceptable forms. Just as frequently, the ideas that get public attention obscure the real economic basis of activities.

One clear example of this is the American Civil War. The generally accepted purpose of that war is that it was a war to end slavery. By analyzing the results and the activities of the people, this idea becomes unacceptable. Slavery only changed form, but not substance, as a result of that war. It did not end until activities by the Blacks—including Thurgood Marshall, Martin Luther King, and Rosa Parks—caused the accepted reality to change. Then there was change. The activities of those who fought the war indicate that there was an entirely different purpose. Immediately after, Fort Sumter, Ohio, raised nine regiments, and two more regiments came from what was later West Virginia. These regiments acted decisively to protect the rail connections on the Baltimore and Ohio Railway through Grafton in what was later West Virginia. The first land battle of the civil war was a decisive move to protect that railroad. It was fought with vigor and initiative at Philippi, West Virginia, under the command of George McClellan, who won such a reputation later for not wanting to fight in the eastern theater. Throughout the war, the people of the Midwest were clearly motivated to protect their economic structure.

This structure required access to markets through states that had access to the ocean. For the people of Ohio and the west, this access was primarily through the port of New Orleans. While the war in Virginia was principally a scholarly exercise in army maneuvering, the war west of the Appalachians was fought without reprieve or rest. Soldiers spent months on the levees opposite Vicksburg rather than go into winter camp. The motivation for such dedication could only be that something important was at stake. That importance was expressed by Lincoln himself when he stated that whether slavery continued or not was secondary to maintenance of the Union. Once the Union was secured and emotions died down, the Blacks were reenslaved under Jim Crow laws, and this was not contested by individuals in the North.

Only when the Blacks chose to make their case, beginning with a school desegregation case, Brown v. the Board of Education, and made themselves heard was slavery finally addressed. The changing of attitudes is not accomplished by war.

The process of integrating differing cultures seems to take about three hundred years. The integrating of the Anglo-Saxons and Normans after the Norman Conquest also took about this amount of time. True integration of Blacks and Whites still has not been thoroughly completed yet.

Typically, the integration of peoples tends to gravitate toward the culture that survives best in the environment in which it exists. Economic structures, then, seem to be controlled by the environment. But environments often allow the survival of different economies. In Alma Ata, a town in Central Asia, exiles with Germanic background continue to maintain clean, neat houses, while local people who live next door have adapted to the sparse surroundings by allowing slovenly conditions to be their way of life.

In the southern United States, two different attitudes toward life exist. Porgy's song, "I Got Plenty o' Nuttin'" from Porgy and Bess is not impossibility, but a well-said reality. Many people whose background is African find that this is the proper attitude to take toward life because in the environment in Africa, a person can only exist by not inviting rats and rot by storing food. So long as the lakes yield fish for supper and food can be obtained easily, this way of life is possible. For people with Nordic thrift, saving food and storing what they need can also exist, and if there is plenty, both ways of life are acceptable.

The problem comes when the environment changes. As food becomes more difficult to obtain, either by increased population or destruction of local food sources, the apparent advantage of one way of life over another becomes a real advantage. In the southern United States in the past, Blacks could live fairly comfortably by fishing for their dinner and taking a relaxed attitude toward life. Whites felt threatened by the ability of the Blacks to exist without the Northern European work ethic. The whites insisted that their children work—and the example of another culture that seemed to be successful without that ethic made it necessary to defend their ideals vigorously.

Blacks who moved to the north gradually understood the advantage that the work ethic gave to those who accepted it. In the north, the accumulation of resources for the winter is not only advantageous, but essential, as is allowing a child to be educated to fit into such a culture.

In the south, the two cultures coexisted, each deriding the other for their silly values. However, as the south became more industrialized, leaders of the Black community realized that something had to be done since the resources that Blacks counted on eventually became less and less available to them. Over time, the recognition that both cultures will work will provide basis for a synthesis. The two cultures can choose what is best of their separate cultures, and a new culture may develop that is appropriate to the region.

SUBECONOMIES

Little fleas have lesser fleas upon their backs to bite'um.
And lesser fleas still lesser fleas, and so ad infinitum.
(Country saying)

When we look at organisms, such as the body, we find that the overall organism is made up of lesser organisms. Lungs and hearts differ remarkably from each other, and eyes and ears differ still more. Each of these parts has its distinct role and organization. Lungs do not pump. Hearts do not have openings to the outside air, and neither reacts to outside stimuli, as do the eyes and ears. Economies have similar differences. There are differences in locations, differences in purposes, differences in available resources, differences in philosophical concepts, and many other differences that set each part of an economy apart from all the others.

This story explains it: A hitchhiker stood at the top of a hill in a gap between Lenoir and Morganton, North Carolina. A driver had given him a ride to that point from Lenoir just as the companies in Lenoir had changed shifts. For five hours he stood and waited for a ride. Every car that approached from Lenoir turned off before it reached him, and the same thing happened to cars coming from Morganton. Not one car drove across the divide. Every driver was part of the economy of the city where he worked. The regional economy of Lenoir did not interact with the regional economy of Morganton. Thus the five-hour wait.

Regional economics is a fact of life in this world and provides for some interesting situations. Textile firms moved to the South from New England in the first part of the twentieth century. The low wages of the Southerners was matched by the low cost of living in the south. New Englanders did not spend the profits they obtained in the south. There, the additional money would compete for the same goods and services and would have increased the price level. This would, in turn, have increased cost. This would have justified a need for increased wages, and that would have destroyed the profit they had developed. The profits were spent in New England. Even though the price level in New England was higher, the additional profits developed by the difference in wages had more value in New England than in the South. Additionally, the increased availability of funding increased the economy of the north.

Regions develop their own levels of resources and needs. At one time, the average wage in the San Francisco area was $9,600 per annum. At the same time, the average wage in North Carolina was $3,500. The items needed for living in each area cost the same proportion of the average wage, even though the actual price was different; for example, diapers in San Francisco were $10.00 for a certain quantity, and in North Carolina, $3.50. Because of the differing revenues and expenses and the same income tax rates in both, the proportion of the revenue left after taxes was smaller in California with a higher income than in North Carolina with about one-third as much income. The North Carolinian was wealthier at one-third the income because the proportions left a greater percentage available to spend. This discrepancy was seldom noted because people were part of the economy of their region and had little knowledge of other regional economies.

Regions in India are far wealthier than in more developed countries. For example, the people of India have more money available to attend movies than almost any other country. With a wage level sometimes stated in the $100 to $200 per year range, they spend more on movies than any other country. Not only is the cost of living less in monetary terms, but the requirements for living are much more favorable. Fuel costs are needed only for cooking, not heating; travel is by the animals they own (and fed from farm production); and needed food is grown on the farm where the people live. This fertile condition makes production of crops less expensive and carries the prosperity to urban areas as well. If the person has a greater percentage of his income free of demand, he is wealthier.

Recall that Charles Dickens described the phenomenon of twenty pounds (or dollars) in and nineteen out as being "satisfaction," while twenty pounds in and twenty-one out was "misery." In demand economics terms, that is the difference between wealth and poverty. This redefinition of wealth has immense impact upon the nature of economics.

The impact also looks at class differences. In northern New Mexico, there are three economies coexisting in the same region that have complete and separate structures. The Anglos, Castilianos, and Pueblos do not interact as one economy but as three. Castilianos are descendants of the original Spanish invaders. The Anglos are English-speaking people who came with the annexation of New Mexico into the United States, and the Pueblos are Indians who were there before the Spanish. The urbanization effect of the minimum wage has eliminated industrialization of the area since it is over fifty miles from any urban center, and freight charges must be paid to send the product to market. North of Santa Fe and across the Sangre de Christo Mountains from any good access to major roads, the isolation of this area is complete.

The Forest Service is the biggest consistent employer and is required by law to pay wages comparable to local industry and wages above the minimum wage. The local wage level in 1963 was well below the minimum wage, so the Forest Personnel Office used the comparable wage for Santa Fe (which was the nearest large town) as their basis for local wage board rates. This created a rate that was far higher for Forest Service employees than were the wages paid by local individuals.

Jacobo Torres was the purchasing agent for the forest. His high wage in the Forest Service made him a major factor in the Castiliano economy. He received his wages in the Anglo economy and spent them in the Castiliano economy. With wages as low as fifty cents per hour, the purchases Jacobo made were percentage of his overall revenues than the equivalent purchases in the Anglo economy and far greater than other Castilianos were able to pay. This tends to indicate that major opportunities for wealth—the difference between income and outgo—are activities that cross the boundaries of subeconomies.

This difference between subeconomies is reflected in the shopping habits of people with differing income levels. High-revenue individuals are expected to shop in high-priced stores. They tend to buy Cadillacs or other luxury cars. The fact that many millionaires shop at Walmart seems to fly in the face of common sense, yet it is reasonable that they have become millionaires by shopping in a different subeconomy.

It is interesting to note that a McDonald's sandwich sold in America for $1 is sold in England for one pound. The price would appear to be proportional to the difference in the value of the two currencies, but each country internally has a proportional equivalency rather than an external equivalency.

By trading between subeconomies, businesses derive a profit for a while. Eventually, they tend to end up being equal so long as structural problems such as isolation do not prohibit this.

LOCAL CONTROL

Subeconomies are defined and separate from each other. One of the most serious difficulties that can occur in an economy is when the control of a subeconomy is separate from its location. Ireland suffered for many years from absentee ownership of the land. People who lived in London and had no contact with the Irish countryside had the authority to determine what was done in the Irish villages. Such influence, no matter how intelligent, must be based on conditions of which those with the authority are ignorant.

In Russia during the Soviet period, any farmer who needed fertilizer to plant a crop had to request it through the channels, many of which led all the way to Moscow. If the requests were approved, the fertilizer might be received some time later, and the crop would be beyond the need for that fertilizer. A major reason for the collapse of the Soviet system was the inability of their subeconomies to manage their affairs locally based on current conditions at the site. There is no assurance that enough information can be received in a distant site to make rational decisions.

In Switzerland, there are gardens where the lowest rows could be planted before similar rows are put in just a little higher. The local climate is that specific in certain cases. When information about what can be done in a specific location is so exact, only the gardener living there can possibility make a sensible decision about what should be done in that garden. In such cases, the idea that someone not at the site could determine what is right for that location becomes difficult to believe.

During Jimmy Carter's term as president, his knowledge about conditions in Georgia was complete, but his knowledge about conditions in California was not. Water projects, which are life and death to many Californians, were denied them because conditions in Georgia did not require such projects. Similar attempts to apply his beliefs about conditions in Georgia when dealing with dissimilar areas were a major reason for considering his presidency a failure. Economic conditions deteriorated because individuals in an area weren't allowed to make the decisions that were needed to support their economy.

The population of Brazil is concentrated in the states with the cities of Sao Paulo and Rio de Janeiro, while less than 4 percent of the population lives in the Amazon Basin. As a result, the people in the large states have the power to determine government policy in the Amazon. Most of these people, having never seen the Amazon, picture it as a lush, fertile area. The reality of the situation is that that lushness is based on the vegetation continuing to grow there. The city dweller is told that he can grow grass where trees now grow and works to obtain land to get out of the barrio (slum) or to expand his farms. When he removes the trees, however, he changes the ecosystem drastically. Without trees, the constant rains wash all the nutrients out of the soil, and the colonist is left with barren subsoil that will produce nothing.

Having committed all his resources to moving to the location, the settler is adamant that he can make the process work, so he moves to a new location. Between timbering for the wood (which is done to satisfy absentee landlord) and this process, the nature of the Amazon is in the process of complete change. Ignorant authority creates many unacceptable conditions.

Local control is not only appropriate in land decisions, but law decisions as well. When the Dred Scott decision was pronounced by the Supreme Court of Judge Taney, it seemed to only imply that ownership of slaves could not be changed simply by moving into a free state. But the people of the free states inferred correctly that, under this precedent, a planter could move to their state, build a plantation, and use slaves to compete with the farmers of that state—so long as the slaves brought into the state had been slaves in the state from which they had come. Such a precedent meant that the Free State laws against slavery were null and void.

Mr. Taney might have used a certain logic then that is accepted today. That logic would have set a precedent that military individuals, serving in Union Service, were under the residency laws of the state where they held residence rather than under the residency laws of the state in which they served. Had Mr. Taney chosen this alternative, the free states would not have fought so hard to overturn the status quo. But the logic used stuck at the very heart of the authority of the state, and the free states could not allow the decision to be effective if they expected to have local control of their affairs.

The importance of the Union to the north was paramount to the survival of the landlocked states of the Midwest. This is shown by Lincoln's reference to saving the Union, regardless of whether the result was slave or free, and by the commitment of the people of those Midwestern states to the continuance of the war. The seaboard northern states, however, would not have allowed the Union to stand if they were required to accept slavery as a nationwide practice. This difference is shown by the attitude of the seaboard northern states to "let our erring brothers depart in peace" and the determination of the Western soldiers to destroy the South by any means available. It was Western armies that ravaged Georgia and South Carolina. Eastern soldiers admired and feared Robert E. Lee, placing a premium on correctness that did not apply in the west. Along with the need for their economy to survive, much of their dedication to completing the war was caused by the need to have the right to make and enforce their own laws.

THE EFFECTS OF STRUCTURAL INTERDEPENDENCY

The health of a subeconomy affects the health of the overall economy, and the structure of the overall economy affects the health of the subeconomy. Your economic health is dependent on the economic health of overall economy. When the overall economy has basic flaws, your economic health will suffer.

The city of Canton, Ohio, has been active in the steel industry for most of its history. As the price of steel has been affected by restrictions on domestic production with costs that do not apply to foreign manufacturing, the health of the steel industry has been deteriorating. Canton steel makers who formerly kept price levels to justify the costs inherent in their methods now command lower prices that do not cover the costs.

As a result, manufacturers who formerly were able to include local taxes as part of the costs of doing business are unable to acquire sufficient funds to provide income to the city, and the city must restrict the use of the remaining funds that they can receive to the services they are able to provide. The health of the subeconomy has been affected by the larger economy.

The opposite is also true. The structure of the overall economy affects the health of the subeconomy.

An illustration in another part of this book describes a doctor from Alaska who purchased a home in North Carolina. He insisted that the price had to be more than the $125,000 that he had received from the sale of his Alaska home. This price was dictated by the income tax provision that exempted tax on the sale of a residence if another was bought for the same or a higher amount within a certain period. As a result, the realtor obtained a listing of an $80,000 home for $125,000, and the doctor paid $45,000 for the privilege of not paying $15,000 in taxes. This structural abnormality has resulted in far more serious economic health problems for the subeconomies involved.

Panaceas have side effects. Now that drug companies can advertise their drugs, the ads that appear are required to list these side effects, and a major part of each ad is dedicated to them. The ads almost seem to be addressed to why a person should not take the drug being advertised. So it is with an economic panacea, but there is no law that requires such a disclosure. The side effects occur, but sometimes are not even observed. As with medicine, too, the result is often to take another drug to offset the effects of the first. Now, under new tax laws, the major investment of most people—"estate"—has been removed from all taxation, and the government must overtax other areas of the economic structure to make up for the loss of estate taxes.

In the Conclusions chapter of this book, we will discuss two possible replacements for this rule. As capital investments, housing costs could be deducted as they are made. As inventory, tax could be deferred. The solution to the problem is to solve the problem rather than add another tax law.

Activity in housing has concentrated on development of upscale housing in place of less expensive homes and helped create homelessness.

Housing materials are "things" and respond to the economic aspects of things. Residences can be sold tax-free. Such tax-free investments are preferred to ones that require tax. As a result, housing activity has increased. That increase, however, has been more in upgrades for people who already have a house rather than in overall housing. A house that only has one thousand square feet of living space costs a certain amount. A house that has seven thousand square feet, often to house only a couple or stand idle to await a buyer, requires seven times as much material. Supplies of things will increase as there is a greater demand for them, but there are realistic limits to their availability. When economic activity is concentrated in certain areas, other areas are either slowed down or cannot continue.

Only so many men are willing to work in the lumber industry, and only so many trees can be grown. These realistic limits, coupled with the increase in supplies that are limited to expensive homes, mean that the cost of a house has increased. That result is not because more people are being housed, but because more material is used in the houses that are built, frequently for those who already have a house. As our population has increased and our housing efforts have been directed to those who already have a house, the result has been a real increase in homeless people and people who live in substandard housing.

Houses deteriorate. Often these houses are homes to people who have lived in them for many years. As the deterioration reaches a point, repairs are needed. The homeowner who finds that he needs a new roof must compete for the services of a roofer who can be paid to either repair his house or a new house that amounts to much bigger and more profitable job than his. To obtain his services, the homeowner must pay his price. Often his resources are insufficient, and the repair is not made.

Take this case: A city code requires that houses be presentable. A man had a house that needed painting or siding. He chose to do the siding himself and bought the materials. The city required that only qualified workers do the siding. The man soon found that his resources would cover either the siding or his food, and he walked away from the house. Our constitution requires that just compensation be made for condemnations, but the city blamed the homeowner for not taking care of his house.

Under the current attitude that anything less than perfection must be changed, we will continue to force our people into the streets. Only an understanding that no process can be 100 percent perfect will overcome this tendency.

CHAPTER NINE

Demand

WHAT IS DEMAND?

DEMAND IS THE accumulation of values that apply to a specific commodity. It is limited by the availability of resources and expanded by the acceptance of goals that allow the use of that commodity.

But demand is not always a function of a specific goal. The first cars invented were not considered useful vehicles, but signs of high status and wealth that displayed how affluent the owner was. That type of demand paralleled the demand for coco-de-mer in India before the advent of western traders. This double coconut was rare and found only when the sea washed them up on the shore. Its rarity gave it value as a status symbol. Individual nuts, the largest known in nature, brought as much as several years' pay when delivered to the wealthy. English sailors found the source of the coco-de-mer in the Seychelles and brought a boatload of it to India. When asked where they found so many, they made the mistake of telling the buyers that they grew on coconut trees in the Seychelles, and the value disappeared immediately. The objective of displaying wealth required that the tokens of wealth be rare.

With this type of demand, the value goes up as the price goes up. People expect that demand will rise with more availability, but as this illustrates, there are goals that do not follow this rule.

The demand curve for any product will relate to
the objective that the product is related to.

The accumulation of individual values that create action is another aspect of demand and is in proportion to the availability of resources that allow action. Resources are limited, and normally, as fewer resources are available, the entity that values the item the most and will give up the most resources to get it wins the right to obtain it. This relationship is comparable to the demand curve.

Car makers started with a demand that is like the demand for coco-de-mer. Certain cars, Ferraris for example, still create more demand as the price goes up. But as more uses for automobiles became apparent, other types of demand developed, until currently the nature of the valuation and the mixtures of various types of demand for a car develop into a part of the negotiation when each car is sold as well as the overall sales of each item.

Demand is related to expectation, not reality. Toy manufacturers plan their Christmas lines in January. At that time, ideas about what people will buy eleven months later can only be conjectured, yet firm commitments to purchase certain toys and not purchase others have to be made. The manufacturers can only gear up to produce the toys that will be sold if they have firm commitments. This period of time from January to Christmas places both retailers and manufacturers at risk for changes in people's preferences. If they don't take this risk, they are out of business. Experience has taught these businessmen that there are ways to reduce this risk, but the risk will always be there.

As more and more subeconomies are included in the mix, these requirements, laid down by the rule of income and outgo, continue to control.

Organisms must eat, and economic organisms must also take nourishment. The time to take nourishment, however, is not continuous but intermittent. We eat breakfast only once a day. At the time for breakfast, an egg has value; the rest of the time, eggs are worthless as a breakfast food. Stability allows us to assign value to eggs throughout the day if there are no eggs available for tomorrow's breakfast. The value of those eggs, however, has a maximum. We will not buy fifty dozen eggs when we will only eat two each morning.

We will acquire the eggs we will need. However, the method of acquiring those eggs may vary from structure to structure. You may raise chickens for eggs, while a friend will buy eggs in the grocery. By choice, you acquire eggs in a manner separate from the economic structure around you, while your friend's is part of that economic structure. There is a transaction to acquire eggs in both cases, but the value takes a different form.

Value is a determination of the ability of the goods or services to satisfy an objective, and it exists before the transaction occurs. Price is different. While the value is often expressed in monetary form, it is not directly related to price. The value of eggs to you is to be found in the willingness to feed chickens and involves no price. To your friend, the eggs' value will result in a price.

To emphasize the point: value exists as a yes/no decision. That decision can be stated as "Do you value what you will receive as greater than what you are giving up?" What you give up has to be less valuable to you than what you receive. For you, the thing you give up is time and care for the chickens. What he gives up is money. If you perceive the time you give up will be more valuable if used in obtaining money, you have the choice of giving up that time for money, and then using the money. In each case, the value I use here is a comparison between two options. Value is a choice between two possibilities.

When I buy a house, there is another consideration to value. The question involves a perception of possibility. If the price needed to acquire the house is greater than the assets I have available to give up, I consider the choice already made for me. When this occurs, I withdraw from the market. I may need a home, but the perceived reality is that I cannot acquire one. This consideration brings out the requirement for a threshold of resources to give up for needs. This idea of the threshold is important because it separates the ability to act from the recognition of hopelessness. Again: the threshold is the point at which a person believes that he has enough resources to take some action.

It is in the best interest of the economy that I have a home, and as a result, the economy develops a method to overcome the idea that I cannot afford it. Mortgages are available to advance the value to allow the purchase. That mortgage is not a gift. I have to determine that I will be able to repay the value advanced. At no time will an economy intentionally allow anyone in it to spend more than he has or can get. This rule—that if your outgo exceeds your income, your upkeep will be your downfall—is an inflexible and controlling rule of economics.

THINGS AND LOCATIONS

When we discussed the nature of objectives in an earlier chapter, we noted that there are different considerations to be understood between things and locations. That is, additional demand creates a will to supply more things. When locations in time and space are involved, the supply is limited. Under our English system of private property, we find that all land is owned by someone. The saying is, "They aren't making any more of it." As a result, land rents are inflexibly related directly to the demand for land. If there is a more valued need for the land than, say, for housing, the same land is reassigned to a different use.

The same applies to time. Every factory worker is limited to 168 hours a week, or twenty-four hours a day and seven days a week. By working overtime, more of that time can be given to acquire funds, but even then, the supply is limited by the need for sleep and nourishment. Moreover, the willingness of a worker to invest more time requires a higher rate of pay than the original and typical forty-hour work week.

A manager has the option of increasing the supply of worker's time in two ways, hiring additional workers, and paying overtime. The first option is a supply of things and the second a rental of time.

Understanding the difference between the two economic factors provides a different approach to a number of economic needs. Health care can be increased by adding more doctors or by increasing the time each doctor spends on the care of patients. We have chosen the worst possible combination of the two in the United States to accomplish health care for our citizens. By increasing the money assigned to health care, we have rented the same doctors' time at a higher rate.

The limit of availability for doctors has kept the availability of the service from expanding. Moreover, even though we insist that a doctor spend many years planning and training to understand a specialty, we insist that he explain every step to an untrained billing clerk before he is paid. Although billing clerks use two guidebooks filled with codes that translate what the doctor puts in his patient's file about the diagnosis and treatment into a number code for the insurance companies, the additional time is still not available for patient treatment. Moreover, those medical situations that are not in the book cause doctors to approximate the diagnosis and choose between possible diagnoses. Since a doctor's time is limited to begin with, the increased demand for his time to accomplish this task, and the task of determining which code will give the better remuneration, further limits the time for treating patients.

At the same time, doctors and universities have limited the possibility of increasing the availability of more doctors by limiting the available places to learn medicine. This limitation still further increases the demand for doctors while limiting the supply. It is notable that there are more internships available for new doctors than there are American candidates for these internships. Foreign students have filled the gap.

It is important to note that the idea that supply will increase if more money is assigned to it will work, but it will work only where there is an ability to increase the supply. The limitation noted above destroys the ability of medical schools increase the supply of doctors. Once the supply is fixed, as in artificial limits on medical training, additional money dedicated to the purpose will only change the balance between available supply and available resource. By increasing the resources when supply is fixed, the result is—and will be—inflationary increase in the cost of these services.

This balance between resources and supplies is a critical understanding. When the economy is working, the size of the economy is not important while the balance is. When the minimum wage was increased from $1 to $1.60 under President Nixon, the cost of all products increased by the same percentage. This increase did not put anyone out of business, but required an increase in revenues and expenses that matched the change. By increasing the minimum wage, the dollar was devalued, but the relationship between income and costs remained the same.

KNOWLEDGE AND RELATIONSHIPS

Knowledge and relationships have different demand curves than do things and locations. Freshmen enter college every year, so the overall demand for teachers of economics remains stable. However, for each student, demand for knowledge is an either-or situation. If a course is offered, only those who feel that they do not already know the subject will enroll.

Relationships have a different demand requirement. Courses that all the students have taken provide a context for communication. If all the students in a party have taken courses under one professor, the conversation may revolve around that professor. Common subjects allow relationships to develop.

These relationships have a balancing element. Coordination of the relationship requires that one person be more dominant than another. Otherwise, the relationship becomes locked in internal problems and cannot face outside objectives.

The subject of balanced elements is revealed here: The Southern Baptist Convention is an outgrowth of Baptist churches originating in Rhode Island under Roger Williams. One of its basic tenets required each person to interpret the Bible in accordance with his own conscience. The problem with this tenet is that no two people would necessarily interpret the same passage in the same way. Baptist churches are notorious for splitting apart over minute interpretations. There is a famous report of the split between the "ice" and "no ice" Baptists in the early 1930s. Air-conditioning was new, and some members did not believe that it was "Biblical" in intent. These "ice" Baptists would not use the newfangled technology. They broke away and formed their own church.

Many of the Baptist churches felt that they could do more in certain areas if they cooperated rather than trying to do the job themselves. They formed conventions in each state and between states. The Southern, American, Conservative, and other Baptist conventions were the result.

Because of Roger Williams's tenet about personal interpretation, however, the convention lacked direction and common purpose. For years, that common purpose arose out of the opposition to alcohol. But as more people came to feel that alcohol was not necessarily evil, that consensus became less useful.

By saying that the Bible was the inerrant word of God and choosing to oppose abortion, the convention found a new consensus. Since no one in his or her right mind would favor abortion as a standard, the objection to abortion was safe. By providing a litmus test about the Bible, they developed discipline. This, a corporate takeover of the Southern Baptist convention, allowed the convention to act in a common manner and established a relationship between the churches that allowed activity to develop.

Relationships allow a common interaction in life. Many resources are devoted to maintaining these relationships.

CHAPTER TEN

Money

MONEY'S ROLE

THE NATURE OF demand creates real problems that require tools for solution. For relationships, one of those tools needs to be a common point of reference. Boats have keels, homes have foundations, bodies have backbones, and economies have money. Money has many aspects. The simplest is as a medium of exchange. By combining or dividing the available money, a value can be quantified.

However, unless there is a common benchmark that can be used to compare an item brought to an exchange, real value is hard to determine. This common benchmark is the understood value of a common commodity. John Keats wrote about the experience of Wendell Fertig in Mindanao during the Second World War in the book, They Fought Alone. Quite a bit of the book deals with Fertig's establishment of a sound monetary system that flourished among the Filipinos and replaced the use of Japanese currency even while the Japanese had military control of the island. Fertig used as his commodity the value of rice and corn, but established a set relationship between the two commodities so that neither was able to create an arbitrage situation between them. Despite the military control of Mindanao, the Filipinos, even the Moros who are such trouble now as supporters of Al-Qaeda, used the monetary policy established by Fertig rather than the Japanese money. When the war was over, the Americans destroyed this currency.

As Keats writes,

> It was (later)… that the war was lost in the Philippines… It began to be lost (when) a soldier…(saw) a…woman (who said.)…"…I will… wash for you."
>
> "…Sure, lady, sure. How much do you want?…"
>
> "Nothing, sair," she said. "Please, enough soap to wash your clothes and mine, only."
>
> She had not intended to ask for soap, for she was to beat the clothes clean on stones in the river bed… He… handed the woman a bar of…soap. The woman's eyes widened….This was…far too much…"Why, with that much soap, there was almost nothing she could not buy from the… Chinese merchant.
>
> But when the woman arrived at the riverbank… her view of the Americanos was subtly changed…she learned that one Americano had paid five pesos for his laundry to done. Five pesos!
>
> It was as much as a man might earn in week!

This woman had a picture of the value of soap and the value of a week or a man's time. Suddenly, the relationships that she pictured as realities were destroyed by the influx of money that had little value to the soldier. Her expectations of stability in the valuation of everything were shattered, and the replacement for those expectations did not fit her community and life.

DISVALUING AND DEVALUING

This is an example of the disvaluing of money. Not devaluing, where the value of money is decreased, but disvaluing—where currency no longer has the ability to act as money. Money that has been devalued retains a relationship, even if it is a different relationship, to a standard commodity. Disvaluing means that money is divorced from any commodity and can no longer be used as a reference for value or as a medium of exchange.

When that norm was destroyed by the indiscriminate spending of the soldiers, the monetary system was destroyed. To this day, the economic system of the Philippines has not been rebuilt. The wealthy take from the peons and demand services in return without paying adequately for them. This same result has historically been seen many times, from the daimyo (or estates of the lords) of the Japanese, to the hacendados of Mexico, to the mirs (a feudal estate) of Russia, and the feudal organizations of the so-called Dark Ages.

Disvaluing money is a major cause of wars. It is not necessary to point to the German economy just prior to World War II. The inflation and disvaluing of the mark caused such distress that any alternative to the situation was preferable to its continuation. I have emphasized the word any in the above circumstance. The German people accepted the Nazis, not because they fully approved of their beliefs and activities, but because the economic situation demanded some amelioration of their difficulties, and the Nazis were available.

The opposition of the Somalis to western assistance during a famine was caused by disvaluation. Farmers who relied on the sale of their wheat could not live because relief efforts were directed specifically to their markets. No farmer can sell wheat where it is being given away for free. The economy could not continue while accepted norms of economic activities are destroyed.

These accepted norms of economic activity constitute the economic structure. In the story above, the accepted norms included a value for soap and for labor. In Somalia, the accepted norm was the value of wheat.

Different commodities have been used for monetary backing throughout history. In colonial Virginia, that commodity was tobacco. As we discussed earlier, that tobacco could be sold in England was guaranteed, and bankers in England would establish accounts that could be used to purchase and ship what the Virginians needed. To ship English pounds to America when trading could just as easily be conducted in tobacco was a foolish waste of shipping space. Not only could tobacco be easily exchanged, but where large quantities were needed for the exchange, the seller would accept claims on the buyer that would be good for a certain amount of tobacco. Such claims became money that was backed by tobacco.

Tobacco did not need to be transferred to be used as money. Recognized claim to the tobacco, evidenced by a chit, note, or memorandum, could be transferred instead. That is, the chit, note, or memorandum served the purpose of money as well. Claims to the right to use money, evidenced by paper recognized as such, are as valuable as the commodity itself. Paper money that relates to the wages a person can earn serves the same purpose—the value of the paper money is understood by the individual earning it and can be related to value of every other need.

It is interesting to note that Virginia and Massachusetts were the hotbeds of the American Revolution because Parliament required payment of necessary official documents in English money. Massachusetts differed from Virginia because it was engaged in trade with countries that were officially off-limits to English subjects. They had plenty of money, Spanish money, but they would have been put in jail if they used it. The states where commercial centers had been established sufficiently to use English money—that is, New York, Pennsylvania, and South Carolina—did not fully support the Revolution until atrocities forced the issue, such as the massacre of surrendered soldiers by Tarleton in South Carolina and by the plight of the farmers on Brandywine Creek in Pennsylvania after that battle. Where no such atrocities occurred, the Revolution was not supported. In New York, the delegation to the Continental Congress abstained from voting for independence to the end.

So some commodity becomes a benchmark in each individual's organization of his or her own life. A good example of this is the factory workers' use of the wage they receive. Because they know they will work so many hours and receive so much money for the time they spend on the job, they are able to use these realities to accomplish so many goals. Certain goals are inescapable—food and shelter are always required—but knowing what resources are available helps them determine whether, if, and how many resources can be allotted to each goal. Within the individual economic structure, the benchmark provides a reference point.

That same reference point establishes the relationship between the individual and the larger composite economic organization. The buyer of a factory worker's time is not paying for the time, but for what that time can accomplish. By the fact that he is required to pay a worker a certain amount for each hour, the buyer can determine what that hour will produce, which allows him to determine his cost. He uses that cost to determine the basic price that he needs to charge to stay in business. For a factory manager, the cost of time becomes a reference point for the price charged to his customers. The price of labor then can be said to be the backing for money.

History seems to bear this out. In 1932, America set the price of gold at $35, but made it illegal for people to own gold as a commodity. Those who used gold could fill their requirements for use, but it stopped there.

Individuals could not use gold as a benchmark for their economic organization under such circumstances. Labor was not the benchmark because labor had little value and could not command the price needed to have that value. During World War II, labor became scarce. Every person was employed. Each person had a supply of a constant, stable, and valuable commodity (labor) then. They had a recognized value for that commodity and knew what it was worth. Because no other commodity had a set value in relation to the dollar, the minimum wage became the backing for the dollar.

The ultimate value of any money in each person's life is determined by what the person can exchange it for. This would be cumbersome in practice, but by having a single commodity, such as labor, backing the currency, all other needs can be compared to that commodity and their value determined by reference to it.

Proof that the minimum wage is the backing for the dollar came during Richard Nixon's presidency when the minimum wage was increased from $1 an hour to $1.60 between March and August. Immediately prices began to climb. Price controls were instituted, but did not work. Only after a summer of escalating prices did the price level stabilize. That stability came when prices were 60 percent higher than before the change. An increase in the minimum wage becomes actually a devaluation of the dollar.

It happens this way. If my salary before the increase in minimum wage change was S1.20 while the minimum wage was $1.00, when the wage was changed to $1.60, I will be unwilling to accept the same wage as another person who was at the minimum wage. I will want to retain the difference between my salary and his. That difference is not twenty cents, but 20 percent of his wage. At $1.60, I will not accept $1.80 as the difference, but will want to be 20 percent above the minimum wage or at $1.92. Each wage earner would go through the same process, so overall wages would advance by 60 percent as well. Since manufacturers will need to increase their prices to obtain the money to pay workers, the price of items purchased will also advance by the same percent. This in effect is a devaluation of the dollar.

All commodities have drawbacks as backing for money. Gold becomes concentrated and unavailable as successful sellers take payment in gold and allow it to accumulate. In 1932, the United States was said to have most of the gold in the world stored in Fort Knox. With this money withdrawn from the financial cycle, that cycle ground to a halt, and the Great

Depression was the result. One of the advantages of the minimum wage as a backing for the currency is the inability of anyone to corner the labor market because every person has twenty-four hours each day, and as long as labor is needed, everyone will be able to make the exchange of their time for currency and participate in the economy.

On the other hand, the mathematical scissors prescribes a maximum revenue that can be expected. Prices are set by the least expensive alternative source that is available to the consumer. With the minimum wage applicable both in the major markets and in the cities that require transportation costs to get the product to the major markets, the additional costs required to transport the product to the market increase the outgo of the economic structure located away from the market. The result is that goods and services that are not "site specific"—not capable of being sold or done at any other place than the site, such as a supermarket cashier—can physically relocate themselves to the major markets. As this continues, even now, Nebraska becomes depopulated, the minimum wage law among the Castilianos who live in New Mexico is ignored (these people, who are so proud of their Spanish ancestry, are willing to work for as little as fifty cents an hour), and jobs paying near the minimum wage cause low-wage individuals to move to the inner cities. Urbanization is a direct result of minimum wage laws that are not ameliorated by such transfers as Social Security, tourism, and welfare.

LOWER FOREIGN WAGES

One of the hardest concepts to understand within an economy is that the price levels are determined within the context of each economy without reference to any other economy. Evidence that the concept is misunderstood is found in the statement "Mexico [or any other country] has an advantage because it has lower wages."

When the textile industry moved from New England to the south, the wages that the mills paid were only slightly higher than the prevailing wages within the same area. Owners of relocated manufacturing plants did not spend the difference between the southern wages and the much higher New England wages. To do this, the additional demand in the south would have raised the costs of their workers and caused them to ask for more money. The savings that the manufacturers realized from the wage differential were spent in New England, where the wage level was already high. This additional spending increased the economic activity in New England so that the loss of jobs by moving the textile mills was offset by the additional activity created by additional funds available in the north.

Should the movement of jobs to another country, however, eliminate part of the costs of doing business, a distinct advantage arises. As I noted previously, a lack of Social Security requirements in Juarez, Mexico, makes the manufacturers who move there avoid locating in El Paso, Texas. By avoiding these costs, the competitive advantage of operating in Mexico becomes insurmountable.

CHAPTER ELEVEN

Economies of Scale

LET'S DEFINE THE TERM

THE CONCEPT OF "economy of scale" has a real effect in economic activity. Essentially, it involves the understanding that there are three separate parts in any activity: preparation, execution, and cleanup. No matter what job you intend to do, there are steps that must be taken before the task can proceed. A speaker must decide what he wants to say. A seamstress must set up the sewing machine. A pianist must open the piano and adjust his seat. A lawyer must know what laws and arguments he can use to support the defense of his client. Each of these actions must occur before the individual gets down to work.

Once these preparatory tasks are accomplished, the activity can proceed, but there is no need to repeat the preparatory tasks every time we repeat the task. So it is that an assembly line can be set up to make cars, and a million cars can be made before another change in the assembly line is needed.

When the last car to be built on an assembly line is made, the assembly line must be disassembled before it can be used again for another model. These three steps—setup, execution, and cleanup—must occur in any economic activity.

PREPARATION

Preparation is a risky step. One retail maxim that works says that "ten by the door, three on the floor, one sale more." Of ten people walking past a store entrance, three will enter, and one will buy something. This ratio sounds very discouraging, but if the retailer failed to provide opportunities for ten people to look his way, he would never make one sale. Commercial real estate agents are taught that not ten but a hundred contacts are needed for one sale. Unless the agent makes those one hundred contacts, he might as well give up.

Venture capital has the same type of risk. New enterprises fail more often than they succeed. The investment in a new venture, such as having a baby, is not a sure thing. Some couples try many times and only succeed sometimes; others must visit doctors or fertility clinics. If the couple feels strongly enough about accomplishing the objective, the risk and outlay is worth the effort. Similarly, the percentage of successful start-ups always represents a low percentage of attempts. When an attempt is unsuccessful, the effort goes straight to waste, another concept that we'll discuss later.

Preparation does not need to be unnecessarily risky. Take this case of an engineer who decided to enter the dairy business and chose DeLaval milking equipment. DeLaval was working with farmers for many years and found that it required a certain amount of detergent to clean the milking equipment. The engineer was trained to analyze every part of his effort and decided that less detergent would work as well. The equipment did not come clean, and he was never able to get top dollar for his milk. He tried to improve on what DeLaval had successfully developed over many years. There is a saying, "Don't try to reinvent the wheel." When you try to redo what has been successfully done before, much of what you do goes straight to waste.

EXECUTION

Real and sustainable value usually comes from the execution stage of any endeavor. This is the most boring and profitable part of any situation. It is boring because everything involved has been decided by the time the execution starts.

Most intelligent people cannot survive the execution stage of economies of scale unless the activity is short. Because the process has already been decided, the activity involved requires no thought. This creates a boring situation where a repetitive action occurs time after time. People who must have a challenge find themselves unable to do the job. They thrive on thinking, but thinking on an assembly line causes mistakes and waste.

The time it takes to complete an activity can be short or long. By breaking the activity into parts and doing each pat as a separate activity, the necessary steps involved in that specific step become easier to remember. In almost every complex activity, the more repetitions that can occur, the less costly that activity will be.

CLEANUP

When carmakers change models, they retool the assembly line. This involves setting up the assembly line for the new model. Before that can be done, the old line must be removed. This cost is not attributed to tearing down the old line, but to the setting up of the new line. Setup and production costs of any product require that the costs be paid before resources become available from an endeavor. Tear-down costs do not have this requirement. Archeologists do not delve in the profitable workings of ancient civilizations. They study the middens or trash piles of those civilizations. These reflect imperfectly the activities of the civilization studied. Profitable activities consume the things that are useful. What is left is the trash. No one has time or interest in reworking what now has no further economic value.

This part of the "economy of scale" concept creates a real problem for people. Since there is no economic incentive to reclaim or eliminate trash under the economy of scale concept, people have engineered packaging that will preserve the product—and fail to provide for eliminating the packaging once it is no longer needed. Styrofoam that will last for many years, tires that cannot be easily burned or stored, tin cans that will not deteriorate, poisons that will leach into fresh drinking water, and plastic containers that will not disintegrate have made a significant portion of our world unusable, if not unsafe.

The resources that support the first two stages of an "economy of scale" situation are not available for the third. These resources will have been used up before the third stage, teardown, has arisen. Any such resources will need to come from a common determination to address the problem, which means taxes and a willingness to use techniques that are currently unacceptable, such as fire, that will require regulation.

HOW IT WORKS

If two assembly lines were set up for the same model, each would require the same preparation and disposal expense as if only one was built. The costs of the first and third of these steps would now be doubled, even though there is no need for more than the original million produced. Per car, these expenses would be doubled without any increase in profitability.

People look for economies of scale in every endeavor. The efficiency of multiple production is so obvious that individuals try to use it even where it is inappropriate. Education curricula attempt to work with children by using a common set of studies, as if each child learned at the same rate. With thirty children in most classes and some teachers having as many as six classes per day, the temptation to use economies of scale in education creates a situation where unprepared students are frustrated by inability to learn, and well-prepared students are frustrated by having to proceed at the pace of slower pupils.

People attempt to use economies of scale in other ways as well. Pro-life individuals try to eliminate abortion by passing a law. Reasons for abortion can range from allergic reaction to pregnancy (often developing after the first child is older), to many other physical situations, to the belief that parents will be abusive and unwilling to love a daughter who is having a child out of wedlock. Each situation demands that separate preparation and personal resolutions about the issue are needed to counteract the idea of abortion. Each situation must be responded to and a needed action taken based upon the circumstances that exist at the time.

American history is replete with examples of attempts to solve multiple problems with single solutions. Sometimes the efforts have been partially successful. Abolitionists created a climate before the Civil War that made a step forward in the treatment of slaves. Unfortunately, that step was not permanent, and it took another hundred years before integration and respect for Blacks began to be the norm. This did not occur until the Supreme Court ruled in the case of Brown v. Board of Education.

At other times, the effort to apply a single solution to multiple problems has been a distinct disaster. Prohibition was an attempt to do away with the evils of alcoholic excess. The result was the development of a criminal subculture and the establishment of bootlegger mentality.

The obvious benefits of economies of scale are a major consideration of the American dream, but the idea of economy of scale has its drawbacks. The first of these deals with the number of goods and services that can be used to accomplish objectives. When these goods and services are monopolized by the established economies of scale (see the next chapter), there are no objectives available for the structures that would be able to compete with those establishments. Economies of scale tend to eliminate economic structures where objectives are limited. Despite the drawbacks, the values of economies of scale cannot be denied.

Without these reductions in cost, many products could not exist. The man-hours needed to make a car would be beyond the resources of any individual. Just the time required to assemble an auto has been placed at over two thousand hours, and the manufacture of many of the parts is, individually, as complicated as the overall assembly. By mechanization and using mass production techniques, many cars can be available for sale within weeks of the order for them.

Mechanization has made the cost of candles at retail as low as $1.50 for certain types. Craftsmen may have to pay that much for the paraffin to make such a candle. By emphasizing the differences between the craftsman's product and the store's product, many craftsmen can still make and sell specialty candles, but generic candles would cost more for a craftsman to make than the price he would have to pay to purchase them in a retail store. Since the price is set by the lowest alternative price, the outgo to make such candles would be greater than the revenue the maker would receive. This means that effectively, the nonmechanized manufacturer will not be able to continue production.

THE VALUE OF LARGE MARKETS

To have a monopoly in a small market does not spread the costs of setup over as many products as a similar monopoly in a large market. The costs and the prices in this case will be larger in the small market than in the large one. This is the basis for the preference for free trade. However, free trade should not have additional costs for either domestic or imported goods. If taxes, tariffs, benefits, or any other cost is mandated for either domestic or foreign trade without similarly being mandated for the other, then protectionism exists. Protectionism occurs when tariffs increase costs for imports relative to domestic production. Reverse protectionism occurs when domestic production must add taxes or other costs that importers do not pay.

CHAPTER TWELVE

On the Matter of Waste and Risk

WHAT IS WASTE?

WE DO NOT like to waste resources. Often, especially when we have many objectives to accomplish and only so many resources, we avoid waste with great vehemence. Unfortunately, waste is an inherent part of life and cannot be avoided. Moreover, some waste is required, and waste is often the best thing that can happen.

Waste is the use of resources for other purposes than the objectives for which it was intended.

When the resource is time, we are limited to 168 hours a week. When we sleep, the time is not useable for productive activities. Our eating time is wasted too if we want to use it to accomplish some objective. Failure to allow this waste creates far more waste. Some objectives such as sleep are mandatory.

Some waste is elective, but carries a severe penalty when neglected. Homestead Industries in Pittsburgh had a steady market for a valve that was better than any other on the market. They chose to build that valve and spend no money on improving their product. Another company found a better process that produced a superior valve. Homestead's product could not compete, and the company went out of existence. The waste of money in research and development would have allowed them to improve their product and stay in business. The waste was elective but necessary.

But even more waste arises neither by necessity nor election. As money moves from hand to hand, some of it falls between the cushions of the couch. This type of friction in the system occurs at every level of every activity. Companies inadvertently overpay vendors. Theft arises from customers and employees, and time and other resources must be used to deal with such problems. Customers who have stretched their resources to the limit fall ill and cannot continue to meet their obligations. No management will ever be perfect, and mistakes cannot be stopped completely.

The constant losses in the financial cycle as money is lost and wasted create a situation where replacement of money is a necessity. If the lost money were never replaced, eventually, there would be no money circulating at all.

Another source of waste is essential to the survival of any economic system: trial and error and risk-taking to come up with new techniques, resources, and products. The Homestead Industries plight illustrates this point as well. New techniques are always needed when resources tend to become obsolete or used up. Troops of howler monkeys in South America often strip all the leaves from the trees they live in. Before that time, one or two young monkeys leap over to other trees and start eating those leaves. If these young monkeys are not poisoned by the new leaves, eventually, the whole troop moves to that new tree and begins to feed on its leaves. The young monkeys' venture is not without the risk of poisoning, but the whole troop would not survive if it did not risk the lives of the few.

Businesses that do not take similar risks fail. Radio Shack produced a computer called the TRS-80 that was advanced for its time. It did not keep up with the market for computers, and it became obsolete quickly.

ACCEPTABLE RISK

There is a risk that customers will not pay according to their agreement. To sell to only those who are guaranteed to pay means a business must restrict its trade dramatically. If such a company sold only to one hundred customers who were guaranteed to pay, they'd make a greater profit by accepting a risk that 5 percent of their customers would never pay. This might allow them to sell to one thousand customers. At $100 per customer, business could increase its profits from $10,000 to $1,000,000 by risking $50,000 on the nonpaying 5 percent.

The most serious place where this element of risk is currently creating havoc in America is in the field of medicine. Treatments for any diagnosis are predicated on the likelihood that that treatment will react with the disease in such a way that the patient will be better after the procedure than before. But procedures are based upon past experience, and patients are notorious for having different reactions to different stimuli. Betsy is allergic to penicillin, John is allergic to milk, Bill is allergic to peanuts, and I can't eat strawberries. The very diversity of the human condition makes it clear that no two people will react to the same procedure in the same way. The result is that every medical activity runs the risk of an unfavorable result, and people who agree to have a procedure take that risk, regardless of what is supposed to happen.

Having taken this risk, however, and acquiring an unfavorable result, the patient still wants to insist that the doctor be infallible. He is expected to guarantee the process. If a person becomes disabled by the procedure, the doctor is expected to replace the income that the individual supposedly would have earned during his lifetime. The absurdity of determining such an amount is an exercise in arrogant belief, whether in a jury's or anyone else's capacity to make such a determination. Moreover, there is never a provision for any accounting for where the money is used. Here, the 5 percent of the people who have unfavorable results end up costing the rest of us more than the total amount of medical expense that we would ordinarily pay.

The reality that a doctor may be incompetent is still a possibility, but risk management should address the removal of the cause of the bad procedure rather than compensating the individual who chose to take the risk. That is, malpractice lawsuits should be addressed toward removing the doctor from his medical practice until he becomes competent, rather than paying the patient for the patient's own risk-taking.

The problem of maintaining the patient in the best possible condition is an ongoing difficulty, but it is a risk that society must take in order to maintain a sound medical system. For this purpose, then, society should take that responsibility through welfare processes. The money involved would be used for the purpose intended, the amount would be determined as needed, and the saving to society would far outweigh the difficulties of making the change.

CASUALTIES

Waste involves risks, but is not limited to risk-taking. Hurricanes, wildfires, and terrorists cause waste that is never in the victim's control. Some of these occurrences are expected and happen so frequently that the amount of overall risk can be determined realistically, if not with certainty. A certain number of buildings catch fire in any one year. If all buildings pay a percentage of the costs of all fires in a given year, those owners whose buildings catch fire can replace or rebuild those buildings from that fund. This understanding gives rise to the industry of casualty insurance.

Some other casualties are never predictable. These catastrophes, such as hurricanes, must be met with some other mechanism to restore the victim to how he lived before the catastrophic event. Here, no private organization can meet the need for recovery. The government of the United States has developed the Federal Emergency Management Act for this purpose.

The attacks of terrorists fall into this category. There are fools who believe that what God has created, God will reward those who destroy those creations. (The rationale is, if it exists under Christian, Moslem, and Jewish tenets, God must have created it.) While we must deal with this type of destruction, the results are clearly in line with hurricanes: we can't control them, just predict them and prepare for them.

ABANDONMENT

Another source of waste is the lack of economic value in the teardown phase of economic activity. Earlier we dealt with the three phases of economic activity—setup, operation, and teardown. Venture capital can be expected to develop future value. Revenues are available to continue current production.

When an economic activity can be replaced, as in the reuse of an automobile assembly line, the removal of the old line is a part of the setup of the next line for the next product. When an economic activity is stopped, however, without any replacement, there is no economic reason to restore the situation to what it was before. The product cycle, which consists of a move from no value to value and then a return to no value, precludes any economic reason for activity to eliminate waste. Brownfields and dumps are the result of this process. If restoration of the conditions existing prior to the shutdown of a process is an objective of the society involved, then funds must come from some other source than economic activities.

COLLATERAL WASTE AND QUALITY

Restoration of brownfields and dumps would not be necessary if we were not reaching the point where waste impinges on our ability to continue living. When the world population was much smaller, waste was placed in middens. Middens are adjacent to every archeological site and provide the most revealing information about the activities of the inhabitants of the site. Broken pottery and other artifacts are far easier to find in these sites than anywhere else. A new and entirely different thinking about what a civilization leaves behind will be necessary before conditions that currently create far too much waste are dealt with.

Such an attitude is required when designing packaging and other temporary articles that will be used and then discarded. At one time tin cans were closed on both ends with caps. These cans, when crushed, popped off both seals and flattened fully. It became easier to form one end of the can and cap the other. This was considered an "improvement"; thus, the resulting can could only be flattened on one end. When such cans are fully crushed, they still take twice the space that the old cans took and double the space to dispose of them. Other packaging has become more durable and less amenable to compression. The combination of technology and a wish for stronger temporary storage of products created such an expansion of waste products that landfills and other waste disposal has become a major problem in America.

A failure to understand the objectives of the users can create waste among most producers. General Electric Outdoor Lighting Division insisted on quality that would last for twenty years and did not understand why their competitors were able to undersell them in many markets. A review of buyers' habits would have shown that most outdoor lights were expected to be replaced in five to six years. The competition built a product lasting only five years and easily undersold General Electric. This failure to build to the buyers' requirements, and not to the producer's idea of what the requirements should be, cost the company many sales.

John Deere builds a quality lawn mower. Owners can expect to use the mower for fifteen years with few major repairs, and these repairs easy to fix.

Homeowners typically remain in a house for an average of seven years. It is cheaper for them to buy a less expensive mower that will last several years and then buy a replacement than to use money that has a significant present value and then abandon the better-quality mower after only seven years.

The misunderstanding of the requirement of quality is pervasive in our culture. Ann Landers was once asked by a nurse to explain this situation: when shoes were ruined by medicines and other chemicals that fall on them during medical procedure, why was there no inexpensive shoe a nurse could buy for temporary use? Her reply dealt with the fact that good quality shoes were easily available. She failed to note that the quality of the shoes had nothing to do with the problem that the nurse faced. Lower-quality shoes that cost less could have been ruined instead of having to pay for quality that could not last. Quality barrels were designed to be used in dropping napalm on Korean War targets. Pilots repackaged the napalm in Japanese barrels because the quality barrels would not break open when dropped on their target.

There is a role for quality products, but the indestructibility of these products and the overbuilt and overpriced use of quality when it is not needed create a major problem in maintaining these products when they are no longer needed. Quality may be a cause of waste in these conditions.

DESIGN FLAWS

Design failures in more permanent structures can also cause waste. I knew of a certain hospital that hired a firm of excellent architects to build a facility. These architects did an excellent job, except that the matter of maintenance was overlooked. The hospital was designed to meet the needs of the community, but maintenance considerations were not made. Utilities were placed above a solid ceiling and under the floor above. When a pipe broke or a change in use occurred, maintenance personnel had to call in construction experts to rebuild the building where the problem occurred. To maintain these utilities created a very difficult problem for the maintenance employees, and often when a change was needed, three times as much labor was needed as would have been required if the utilities were easily accessible.

The example that the Boeing Company provided in the building of the 777 aircraft was, and should be, followed in cases like this. Here the full design was made on a computer long before any physical work was started. Input from users and others who worked with the product then or would work with it in the future was elicited. This allowed their designers to reduce this type of waste. For example, the time wasted in starting up a computer could easily be reduced if unneeded components of the operating system could be safely eliminated.

Waste is a pervasive and necessary part of economic life, but it cannot be funded from ordinary economic activity and should be dealt with in the designing and producing of products.

Understanding and dealing with the element of waste, both as a necessary ingredient of economic activity and as a problem for future activity, are essential.

CHAPTER THIRTEEN

The Inevitable Monopoly

WHY INEVITABLE?

Every economic activity, unregulated, becomes a monopoly.

THAT ACTIVITY MAY become a monopoly by income, efficiency, subsidy, power, legality, positioning, deep pockets, or information, but whether or not the economic activity calls itself competition, it will become a monopoly if it is unregulated.

Whenever people are willing and eager to pay less than the full economic costs of any economic activity, they are causing a monopoly to develop.

Whatever people think they can do to avoid a monopoly, the nature of economics rules. It overcomes their good intentions. Unless people choose to avoid monopoly and act upon that choice, monopoly or exclusive possession is inevitable.

HOW IT WORKS

Suppose two men are barbers. Mr. A owns his shop, and Mr. B must pay rent. Mr. A also has a pension and stocks. He has no need for the revenue from his barbershop. When this happens, Mr. A can charge only ten cents for a haircut, and Mr. B, in order to justify having his shop and earn a living, must charge a far higher amount. Under these circumstances, Mr.

B could not exist as a barber if there were not a union or some regulation requiring Mr. A to charge a reasonable amount since Mr. A can set the price for a haircut as low as he wants to.

Some years ago, lawn mowers had no "deadman" mechanism to stop the mower when the user was not at the controls. A law was passed requiring such a mechanism in order to reduce the number of accidents with lawn mowers. A mechanic was asked if the law was not a nuisance, since it eliminated the old type of lawn mower. His response was that there would never be the new type of lawn mower without the law, since the makers could never be assured that they could recover the costs that were needed to make the deadman mechanism.

These examples illustrate the nature of the simple rule that is violated when people look out only for a lower price. Competition cannot exist without price regulation. The idea that competition can exist if the supplier cannot recover his costs is ludicrous.

When the airlines were deregulated, Eastern Air Lines had no monopoly at any airport. The prices for the flights on all the routes Eastern flew were set by the airline that could continue to fund the wages of the employees, the amount of gas needed, and the maintenance of the airplanes. Airlines such as USAir in Pittsburgh, which had a monopoly on certain routes, could increase their charges on flights originating at that airport and subsidize the competitive routes. This allowed them to set their price as low as they wanted on competitive routes.

The result was that the least vital of the three variable costs of an airline's flight was cut to allow the planes to remain in the air. The most spectacular result of the reduction in maintenance, in order to continue flying, was the loss of the cabin on a Hawaiian Airlines flight. Although there was no cabin to keep the passengers safe, the plane landed with everyone still strapped in. They had enjoyed a scheduled flight in the open air for the first time in aviation history.

In these circumstances, Eastern Air Lines's income became less than its outgo. It could not fund the ordinary expenses of the flights, and it failed.

Currently, the price of airline tickets is at the mercy of the airline. If they have a monopoly, as TWA once did in St. Louis or Northwest in Minneapolis, the price of the ticket originating or ending there is far higher than a comparable ticket between competitive airports.

While they are revealed in the history of England and China, as well as other historical entities, the problems associated with the concentration of wealth are not seen immediately. In England, the accumulation of wealth during the Hundred Years' War was succeeded by the anarchy of the Wars of the Roses, followed by the accumulation of wealth during the Tudor reigns, the anarchy of the Civil War, etc. This cycle covered a period of centuries. The history of China consists of the recounting of the cycle from peace to plenty to concentration to anarchy. Monopoly can and should be controlled to avoid the same result in our history. It is a long-term problem. Within the lifetime of any individual, the situation will appear to be stable, but over time, the cycle becomes inflexible.

We have seen one solution to the expected anarchy in the chapter on monopoly. It is essential that the concentration of wealth not destroy the health of the subeconomies of which the national and world economies consist. Should those subeconomies prove to be unprofitable to the individuals and families that use them, they have no choice but to become enemies of the overall economy.

MONOPOLY BY INCOME

Any difference in income will tend toward monopoly. An example will show what this means. John has an income of $20,000, while Bill has a salary of $30,000. John and Bill have the following expenses each month:

	John		Bill	
	Monthly	Annual	Monthly	Annual
Rent or house payment	325	3.900	400	4,800
Food	500	6,000	600	7,200
Automotive	450	5,400	525	6,300
Taxes	200	2,400	300	3,600
Other	200	2,400	300	3,600
Total		$20,100		$25,500

John with a salary of $20,000 has to pay out $20,100, while Bill with $30,000 has a $4,500 surplus.

John has to borrow to cover the extra $100 while Bill has $4,500 that he can spend as he chooses. This happens even though Bill has spent significantly more in every category.

One way that John can cover the additional costs is to borrow, and Bill has money to lend. Now John has the additional cost of interest to Bill, and Bill has additional resources. This disparity is inevitable unless there is a willingness to avoid it.

This difference occurs not because Bill is avaricious, but because percentage math and absolute math do not work in the same way. Absolute math has a tendency to increase without limit or decrease the same way. On the other hand, both a top limit (100 percent) and a bottom limit (zero) limit percentage math. Income is controlled by absolute mathematics, while outgo is controlled by percentage math. While your income can be increased or decreased without limit (bankruptcy occurs when it goes below zero), outgo is controlled by income. No one can spend what he doesn't have or can't get.

As Bill continues to have a surplus and John continues to be forced to borrow from Bill, everything John has, eventually, becomes owned by Bill. Bill has a monopoly by virtue of his income.

MONOPOLY BY EFFICIENCY

There are never two processes to create a product that have exactly the same costs. Differences in cost can develop in many ways. Location, processes, materials, taxes, energy, abilities, knowledge, capital investments, and even appearance can cause differences in the costs of any product.

If there are two locations, one near the market and one far from the market, the one far from the market must incur transportation costs to sell its product. The remote location has other difficulties. FedEx does not deliver by ten o'clock in the morning to Canjilon, New Mexico. The distance from either Santa Fe or Farmington requires too much drive time, and the volume of deliveries does not justify flying. The liability of living in remote locations creates a situation for those residents where wages are so low that minimum wage laws are either ignored or no economic activity occurs.

The increased cost of getting to market results in local businesses within the market area to have monopolies of equivalent products.

The process a business uses can never be exactly equal to any other process. Candles manufactured by a craftsman will always cost more than mass-produced candles. Even two craftsmen will have different ways to craft their candles and will have differing costs because of those discrepancies.

Candle craftsmen do not develop monopolies, however, because they are never able to produce enough candles to fill the need. Mass-production methods, on the other hand, can produce that amount. No matter what job I set out to do, there are three stages to it (see the preceding chapter). The first is preparing the scene, finding the tools, and setting up the operation. The second is the job itself. The third is putting things away and cleaning up the site. If I make one thing, the setting-up and tearing-down costs are a certain amount. If I make two things while I'm at it, there is no additional cost of setting up or tearing down. If I make fifty, there are some additional costs, but not many. Where there is such an economy of scale in a process, that process will eventually overcome any similar process without it. Whenever a method of production becomes efficient enough to supply all the needs for their product, it will become a monopoly.

The availability of materials becomes a reason for differing costs and a monopoly by equal revenue with smaller costs. A business that has access to plastics that are equivalent to steel at a fraction of the costs will eventually have a business advantage that will result in a monopoly if the owner of the business chooses to do so. Phelps Dodge was a company that mined copper. Copper wire was far easier for them to manufacture than for a business that had to buy copper from them. Wire manufacturing by Phelps Dodge brought the price of wire down to the point that others were forced out of business.

OTHER TYPES OF MONOPOLIES

Sometimes monopoly occurs because of subsidy. The airline industry once was regulated. No carrier could charge less than the full cost of the flight, according to legislation. They could compete on service, on options, on efficiency, even on ambience, but they were prohibited from charging less than the direct cost of flying the planes. That direct cost consisted of gas for the flight, payroll for the attendants, maintenance of the planes, and several smaller items. Where airlines had a monopoly in an airport, there was no need to charge large sums for flights, and if the airline did, competition would be able to establish itself there.

Then deregulation went into effect. Airlines that had monopolies in specific airports increased their prices there and used the additional money available to them to subsidize flights in competitive markets. These flights did not return enough money to pay for the gas, payroll, and maintenance of those flights, but other airlines had to meet the price they set. Take such airlines as Eastern, whose case was mentioned earlier. All of Eastern's routes were competitive, and they were forced to fly at prices that did not cover the cost of the flight. Since they could not spend more than they had or could get, they found they could not continue to fly and went bankrupt. By subsidizing prices that undercut the competition, monopolists destroyed that competition.

Sometimes power is the cause of monopoly. We think of power as being the ability to force someone to do as we want him or her to act. This type of power has been frequently used historically. Thinking this way, we can look to the situation in Ireland in the nineteenth century. There, the power of English arms required the Irish to pay rent for the land they lived on. Absentee landlords received the rents even though they were not required to provide any maintenance or improvements to the property. In Medieval France, the king gave a monopoly on the sales of salt to some of his courtiers.

Sometimes monopolies are encouraged legally. Patents are legal monopolies. Synthroid is a high-profit synthetic hormone used to replace natural hormones provided by the thyroid. Recent attempts to reduce the costs of this drug, essentially a patented commodity that is essential to the health of the people, resulted in a class-action judgment against the company.

Frequently in the past, legal authorities have assigned a legal monopoly for some commodity, such as the mail. Only after the laws were changed did UPS and FedEx, private shippers, become able to deliver letters.

Early positioning in the area where the monopoly develops can cause it. AOL has a major position in the Internet access business, despite the failures of their systems to allow for essential programs to coexist with theirs. They were the first to issue methods for people to use their system, and by the time more efficient systems were in place, customers had already committed to them. AOL's procedures are not as efficient as other Internet providers, but their position in the market precluded competition or a period of time.

Monopoly can occur because there is money or another resource too finance it. The Dutch West Indies Company was formed after the Dutch East Indies Company had returned from Indonesia with products that yielded 200 percent profit. As a result, the management felt they had to return equal results to compete with that company. The profits from New Amsterdam, Recife, Brazil, the Dutch West Indies, Aruba, Bonaire, and Curacao did not justify the payments they made; therefore, they had no money to defend these territories. All but the ABC Islands are now in other hands. The Dutch East Indies Company, with far greater profits, even with the higher dividends, lasted until World War II.

In the airline industry, Delta, with its policy of avoiding debt, has held its own, even though the industry has completely different rules to live under. With the money available to remain in business, it has stayed strong even as others failed, although this has changed recently.

Ability to obtain information can cause monopoly. Near the end of the nineteenth century, Jay Gould owned Western Union, the business that controlled the telegraph at a time when it was the only way to send information rapidly. He required his operators to inform him of messages sent by other companies with information he needed to keep his edge. By using that information, he frequently gained control of the other companies.

Monopolies are inevitable in any stable economy. Mathematically, they are the norm when any industry is able to supply the entire product that is needed. There are no natural checks on their progress, and frequently, they are the most desirable result of economic activity.

MONOPOLY IN AN ORGANISM

An organism is a unit that is stable, has activities, interacts with the environment around it, has organization, has parts that contribute to the whole, requires nutrition, and produces some effluent. An economic system fits all these requirements. The idea that economic systems have organic properties gives a different point of view to many aspects of economic thinking.

Monopoly is an ordinary part of any organism. A person has only one stomach, one brain, one heart, etc. When elements of the economic system are properly in check, monopolies are to be preferred to excessive competition. The problem arises when any one monopoly has such stability that it attracts most of the resources to it. By accumulating resources in one par, these resources are denied to other parts. As these other parts starve, they cannot accomplish their function, and in some cases, the organism dies. In one organism, the body, that result is called cancer, and it will destroy the body.

An example of economic cancer is not so old. John D. Rockefeller arranged for the oil business to be a monopoly. The reasoning behind his effort is not too hard to figure out. A producer could take his product to market on Monday and receive a high price for it. That sale would be all the market could absorb that day, and there was no demand for oil on Tuesday. Then another producer would take his oil to market and have to pay all the costs without any funds available because there were no buyers.

By establishing a monopoly in oil, Rockefeller's organization assured the producer that when he brought his oil to the market, he would receive $28 for each barrel he produced. With the assurance of a stable price, oil then could be produced by anyone.

It developed this way.

Before the Civil War, Americans were dedicated to the land, and their resources were directly related to making the land produce. This enabled a certain equality to exist between the economic structures of the citizens. The cooperation and organization that the Civil War developed allowed a different arrangement of economic organisms. Merchandising and manufacturing, such as the production of oil, became far more secure means of acquiring resources than farming. Agriculture has always been an unstable source of resources since the weather can change production drastically any one year. The new methods were far more stable.

During the war, the economies of the towns where the soldiers had lived before the war adjusted to their absence. That adjustment eliminated the roles that the soldiers would have normally played in the economic activities of their homes. This required them to look elsewhere for a means of acquiring resources.

One such way was to make use of things that were formerly considered of little value. In Titusville, Pennsylvania, there was oil available, but it had not been fully exploited. People began to take this oil to market. There was not a developed market, so chaos ensued. A barrel of oil might sell for $50 one day, but when the next barrel arrived in town, there might be no buyers. The seller then had to pay for the transportation as well. Such a situation was not in anyone's best interest.

John D. Rockefeller, with others, worked to end this chaos, and eventually there was a set price for oil. This price was maintained for twenty years. With the set price, stability came to the industry. That stability attracted investment capital. Continuing capital investment in the oil industry and other stable industries eventually meant that sources of capital for other purposes, such as agriculture, could not be found. In the same way as cancer works in the human body, the accumulation of funds in the stable industries deprived the remainder of the economy, starving it. There was a reaction against "trusts," which were organizations that had control of these monopolies. Monopolies were considered to be robbing the poor and defenseless, and breaking them up became the order of the day.

This effort to break up monopolies was not carried as far as the rhetoric indicated. The catchword monopoly was used to build up support for the actions that were taken, but no one expected that the oil industry, for example, would be destroyed. The oil industry was efficiently run as a monopoly even with its excesses, but the more serious problem was that it absorbed too much of the available usable wealth. Again, when the percentage of wealth is controlled by the monopolies, the remaining wealth is insufficient to fund essential activities in other businesses.

Every economic organism deals in percentages of its total resources. This holds true of each part of an economic organism. When economic organisms as a whole are reviewed, you can see how percentages are in control there as well. If an individual must pay double the amount that he anticipates for food, unless his resources increase, he must reduce the amount he can pay for clothing or housing or other expenses. When that reduction eliminates enough resources for the vendor, he also must eliminate expenses. At some point, he must cease operating at all.

When we discuss the Depression, we will find that available funds in New York were less than the expense required for truckers to haul food from Florida. When this happened, produce rotted in Florida while people starved in New York.

Comparing the economy to the human body is an easy possibility. Every healthy organism provides all that is needed for each of its parts. In the body, the stomach and intestines provide nourishment. The blood vessels take nourishment to each part of the body and return what is not needed for disposal. The eyes, nose, and other senses provide information to the brain to coordinate the organism's activities with the world outside.

Each part has a role to play, and when the parts are working well, the body is healthy.

How can the body become unhealthy? There are several ways: nutrition may be absent, some part may fail, the brain may give faulty instructions, other control methods may fail, preference may be given to one part that aggressively acts independently, and other problems may arise.

An economy can starve. Between the First and Second World Wars, Germany was required to send a major part of its production to the Allies in reparations. What was left was not enough for the people to share equitably. Bidding for the remaining food left many people out in the cold, and inflation was such that a person could not buy what he needed to exist. Germany starved.

In a body, some part may fail. Diabetes is the failure of the pancreas to produce enough insulin. That failure does not allow the cells to use what is available to them. Education may serve society in the same way. If an education system encourages individuals to place their individual interests before the interests of all, both the individual and the society fail. If a musician cannot learn to play an instrument, there is no music. Other parts of society serve the same type purposes and can fail in the same way.

As the brain may give faulty instructions, so may governments do the same. When governments idealize some concept that is not related to reality, the consequences can be destructive. The Nineteenth Amendment banned alcohol. The consequences that arose included destruction of many breweries, development of gangs, and a pervasive attitude that crime was something to be looked up to, almost fun.

Other control methods may fail. The body has hormonal controls that have nothing to do with the brain directly. In society, such groups as churches serve the same function. When the churches choose to isolate themselves from the needs of the people, they become irrelevant. Churches that serve only the needs of the wealthy, for instance, and eliminate those who have little find themselves dying as the wealth of their parishioners diminish or the wealthy move away.

Preference and independent aggressive action creates monopoly. In the body, this is known as cancer. The same thing happens in society when individuals become so wealthy that they can ignore the interests of all others. Paul Allen of the Microsoft Corporation bought an island that had been the campground of the Boy Scouts, evicted them, and built a house that is far more than he needs. He had the power and felt he had the right to destroy the community for his own personal preferences. This is a real problem with monopolies.

THE GOOD THINGS ABOUT MONOPOLY

That there are problems with monopolies is understood, and if left alone, monopolies starve all the other parts of the economic body. This would indicate that monopolies should be avoided at all costs. The body, however, has only one heart and one of each type of organ that does not require the cooperation of the sets of two, such as ears, eyes, and limbs. Over time, societies tend to concentrate their means of living to one industry or product as well. Intrinsically, in almost every example, economic activity tends toward monopoly, leading us to conclude that there is something inherently beneficial about it.

Where more essential production is necessary, mass production techniques will make goods and services more readily than individual attempts. Each individual attempt must include all the costs of setting up manufacturing. The monopoly reduces the need for those extra costs, as we discussed in chapter 13 on the economies of scale. To benefit from this advantage though, mass production requires a stable market. Stability in a market can come in several ways. Monopoly provides the ability to limit production to what is needed. Cooperative marketing works well where rogue sellers are avoided, and governmental regulation can work as well.

As an example noted earlier, the manufacturers of lawn equipment had no "deadman mechanisms" (a safety feature) on the machines they manufactured. No manufacturer was willing to put this additional safety feature on their machines because they weren't assured that anyone would pay the additional cost required for the installation of the part. No investment will be made where the amount invested will never be recovered in some type of value. Where the value involved can only be expressed in money, the additional costs that others will not pay demands that the investor not make that investment. The change was made only when regulations required every lawn mower maker to put deadman devices on their product. Monopoly allows such production.

The benefit arises when economies of scale and specializations are considered. Every enterprise involves the costs of initiation—research, development, tooling, finding markets, training, etc. None of these costs by themselves benefits anyone. Venture capital is required to cover these costs. It is frequently the basis for loss, and unless there is some assurance that the venture will succeed, there is little value assigned to it.

The computer technical stocks recently had a great deal of value assigned to them. Yahoo, the Internet provider, had stock that advanced from $17 to over $180 as it showed how Internet selling and advertising could return an investment. When it became obvious that the promise would not be fulfilled, technical stocks as a whole (the NASDAQ index) fell from over $5,000 to less than $2,000. Start-up costs in any industry can only be recovered if there is enough perceived value among investors so that customers will pay enough to replace their investment.

Every company has fixed costs that cannot be eliminated and continue whether goods and services are sold or not. Banks must have employees and record-keeping requirements, whether there is any money to lend or not. These costs are the same for each banking company. When banks expand services, the same revenues must cover the new services as well. Competitors who do not have these additional services keep the bank from increasing its revenue. Frequently, banks merge to overcome this difficulty. Eventually, these mergers become a monopoly, but the services of the bank continue.

So the benefits: monopoly is the efficient way to accomplish any objective. There will always be sufficient revenue to provide for all the costs, since there is only one place that the product can be obtained, and the cost must be paid. Research and development and other costs that would not be possible if only the lowest cost were paid can be insured since competition will not drive the price of the product below cost. In an economy, as in nature, monopoly is the best solution.

THE HISTORICAL CYCLE

One of the most insidious problems in any economy is the tendency for concentration of wealth. When wealth becomes more and more available to fewer and fewer people, more and more economic structures become unable to meet the requirements that allow them to be active, especially the requirement that they have resources. The saying that great wealth begets great poverty refers to this phenomenon. Its truth can be demonstrated at many times and in many ways. Although vintners say, "The way to make a small fortune in wine is to invest a large one," we are not talking here about the poverty derived from a bad investment. Instead, we are talking about the fact that concentration of resources forces those left behind out of the economy.

Brazil is noted for its wealthy farmers and its shanty towns called favelas. People can exist in a shanty town, but do not have the threshold amounts of income that allow them to contribute to the economy of which they are a part. Monopoly denies them the right to contribute to it. Without this threshold amount, the people end up doing whatever they can, and as they have nothing to lose, they tend to act criminally. Because of this, the wealthy have to spend more money for police and security that is not needed elsewhere.

When things get to a certain point, people have to change the situation or starve. They rebel, and destroy all that they think has caused them pain. This reaction lasts as long as the memory of those problems is alive in the participants. Now the pain is in anarchy, and people are willing to reestablish stability. The stability allows concentration, and the cycle repeats itself.

The histories of many countries bear this out. China has a long history, and in that history, there is a continuous alternation between the concentration that develops from monopolies in a stable situation and the chaos and revolution that occur because of the need for relief from such concentration. Mexico and other Spanish-American countries have the same pattern of stability and chaos. England had its stability during the Hundred Years' War, anarchy during the War of the Roses, and stability under the Tudors, followed by the English Civil War. Where stability prevailed for long periods, an inflexible social system developed that restricted everyone to specific roles. Such a system arose in Japan. Prior to the opening of the country to the west in 1854, the country was divided into daimyos, whose lords designated a specific role for every citizen. If the citizen chose not to fit into that role, he was subject to death.

The puritan work ethic assumes that there will be work available for all people. It looks down on those who do not work and assumes that failure to work is a fault of the individual. Unfortunately, there are many times when there are no objectives that need to be met by those who have resources that can be used. Even more frequently, the resources needed to accomplish a job are both beyond the resources of the individual and redundant for less expensive means of fulfillment.

As means of production become more concentrated by the inevitability of monopoly, more and more people become unable to obtain the resources that are needed to contribute to the economy of which they are a part. When the situation becomes too extreme, the people who are pushed out of the economy find that morality becomes too expensive for them. These people, like the thief Pedro Cabral in Mexico City, find other means to survive. Such thieves and pickpockets are the result of these people discovering that such work is far more rewarding than legitimate endeavor.

The United States has been able to overcome this propensity to move to more lucrative but immoral means of obtaining resources by its development of Social Security and other welfare programs that enable individuals who have no resources to remain in the economy. The vast profitability of the drug trade, however, has lured many individuals to invest in and profit by the high returns on their money that increase their resources. As long as the efforts of the people in charge are directed to moral arguments rather than toward the profitability of the trade, the attempts to end the trade are doomed to failure. As long as the price of the drugs is astronomical, the pushers will continue to entice individuals to try the drugs. Once onto drugs, the pusher is guaranteed that the user will not turn them in since then, his source of supply will be cut off, and he will have to suffer the punishment of withdrawal.

The efforts of China to stop the drug trade during the opium wars show that enforcement of drug laws will never be the answer. The limitations on the supply of drugs actually proved to be counterproductive since they increased the price and assured the pushers of a higher profit. Given that morality is irrelevant in this situation (remember the second digression), it becomes necessary to assure the user that he will not be harmed by drug laws. When he becomes able to believe this, he will be in a position to cooperate with those laws.

If there is ever a serious effort to eliminate drugs, it will include providing drugs at a reasonable price to those who are unable to withdraw, incentives to users and others to inform authorities of actual situations, and a destruction of the profitability of the drug trade. A possible solution would be to provide drugs at a reasonable price, such as twenty-five cents per dose, and an assumption that any sale above fifty cents is an illegal act, for which confiscation of all assets of the seller is a penalty. These assets would be placed in the hands of an executor, who, for a reasonable fee, would maintain the assets until the determination of whether they would be permanently confiscated. Any funds that the perpetrator required would be determined by the trustee. Upon verification that the confiscation should be permanent, any informant would be given a reasonable portion of the estate for his assistance. With a program that deals with the problem realistically, the drug trade may be stopped.

The use of prison space and time is counterproductive in this case. Limiting the location of the prisoner while providing him with the resources he needs to survive causes no problems as long as he can communicate with those who will benefit by helping him. The restrictions on his movements are not a great problem for him. By coordinating the efforts of others or funding the investment needed to push drugs, his economic structure is strengthened rather than punished.

In this instance, the economy of scale in an industry is a major cause of its success. Routes to import drugs into the United States require a great deal of setup costs. Protection of couriers requires preparation. The expense of this setup can only be supported by highly profitable enterprise. Luckily for the pushers, the product is homogenous, easily transported, and vital to the physical and mental well-being of the user. Just as tobacco provided a secure, safe, and constant value to the colony of Virginia, drugs provide a constant value to the drug pusher, which can be secured by appropriate payoffs, made safe from competition by drug laws and safe from treachery by users finding alternative sources at reasonable prices.

To repeat, in almost every historical period and country, the cycle of chaos, stability, monopoly, and chaos can be found. America had its Shays' Rebellion (armed farmers rebelling against mortgagers) establishment of the constitution, monopoly under Biddle's bank, chaos under Jacksonian Democracy, a period of stability, intersectional rivalry, stability after the Civil War, monopoly under the robber barons, anti-trust actions that delayed the chaos of the depression, stability that developed after World War II, and monopoly that has created such envy that terrorist actions are now attempting to create chaos.

This is an inherent cycle in history.

HOW TO DEAL WITH MONOPOLIES

Because the solution to this problem can be understood here, we are including it. We will repeat the solution in our conclusions.

There is no possible reason for people to pay excessive prices for monopolistic products. The monopoly is as stable as the government, and we have a benchmark in government financing. When governments borrow money, they must pay a certain interest rate. Monopolies have no reason to earn more than the government and should be limited to that yield on their sales. A monopoly should be limited to earnings (including payments to officers who can decide what will be spent) of no more than the yield of government bonds if the goods or services provided by the monopoly are essential to the health of the economy. If government bonds and monopolies have similar characteristics and risks, there is no reason that the investments in each should not be equivalent.

Such a rule applied to essential goods and services—with a definition of monopoly that makes sense—would hold the problem of overpayment for services in check. This would not include, for example, ornamental diamonds, which cannot be said to be essential goods. Such a definition could be that a monopoly exists when 50 percent of the production of a product is handled by one company, or 70 percent by two companies, or 90 percent by three companies.

The significance of the inherent cycle of chaos, stability, monopoly, and chaos must be dealt with to finally break the cycle.

CHAPTER FOURTEEN

The Current Nature of Value

PAST VALUE DOESN'T COUNT

THERE IS A story of a doctor whose father asked him for a loan of $1,000. The doctor refused the request. The father asked him why, arguing, "I conceived you, raised you, educated you, and set you up in practice. Why can't you loan me the money?" The son replied, "I know that you conceived me, raised me, educated me, and set me up in practice, but…what have you done for me lately?"

The expectation of willingness to repay his father makes this a very macabre joke. We do invest in our children and expect them to reciprocate. But this is an investment, not an expectation of quid pro quo. In economics, the story is not macabre or even unexpected. Value is always a comparison of current value of one item to the current value of another.

SOME EXAMPLES

During World War II, people bought war bonds to help the war effort. Immediately after, prices began to climb. Values of consumer goods in the fall of 1946, one year after the war was over, commanded half as many dollars as the same consumer goods four years later. What could be bought with the savings that were represented by war bonds was reduced in value by half. The current relationship of the dollar to what could be bought in

1946 did not compare in any way to the relationship of the dollar to what could be bought in 1950.

The difference between the idea that economics deals with the current situation and our wish for investment to succeed is a subtle one. We like to believe that what we save can be spent later. Since time immemorial, people have been surprised when their savings have not held their value, but the realities of economics are that what is valuable today is valuable only in the context of today.

For example, the idea that Social Security is a matter of savings for retirement is a fallacy. By tying the payments to current earnings of wage and salary workers, the current value of the payments insures that those payments are a portion of current spendable income that has a constant relationship to overall spending by the general populace. Money that has been taken from a worker's wages is not saved and then returned to him. The money that he and his employer pay into the system is paid to another person, sometimes a retiree, sometimes a disabled individual, and sometimes to a minor child. Upon retirement, the worker will not receive the money he has paid out, but his share of the current earnings of other workers. Since the percentage of spending by individuals who rely on social security remains constant, whether the level of wages goes up or down, the ability of the recipient to continue to participate in the current economy continues and in a proportionate manner.

Recent efforts by many individuals to tie Social Security to savings and investments fail to notice that savings remain constant when prices levels change. A person with bonds with face value of $50,000 in 1945 would have needed another bond of the same amount to make an equally valuable purchase in 1950. Over five years, the price of anything that could have been bought in 1945 had doubled. On the other hand, an airline pilot who retired with a stock pension in 1974, designed to last his lifetime, found that stock prices in 1975 had declined so precipitously that the fund was exhausted in the following year.

Investments are just that, investments. The investment a mother makes in a child causes her to protect that investment in every way possible. When the investment turns sour, as when the child becomes a criminal, most mothers find that they are unable to accept the loss of the investment and fight to protect the child, even when he is clearly wrong. Investments are an attempt to use resources that are available and not restricted so as to increase other resources. Some are successful, others are not, but they are never in any way related to the current level of continued spending. Since these investments are also not related to the current value of money, their value increases or decreases independently of any other economic consideration. Savings are necessary to provide resources for future activities but, once put to use, take on a life of their own.

At any time, the perceived value of things that can be purchased is equal to the perceived resources that can be used to purchase them. Earlier chapters have dealt the mechanism by which resources are apportioned. In every circumstance, the apportionment is only valid in light of what can be done at that specific time.

TIMING

We previously discussed the anarchy that existed in the oil industry just after the Civil War. Until John D. Rockefeller and his friends stabilized the industry by developing a monopoly, a person could produce a tank car full of oil and did not know whether there would be a buyer when he reached the market or not. This unreliability of the market precluded mass production. In almost every case, production does not exist if markets are uncertain. To overcome this difficulty, contracts provide certainty that an item that is manufactured can be sold, but the element of timing is always present to some degree. Hula-Hoop manufacturers were able to sell their product only as long as the fad continued. When the fad stopped, the demand disappeared—suddenly.

OBSOLESCENCE

For many years, American Motors manufactured a car that lasted far longer than any other manufacturer's car. Despite the quality of the product, American Motors found itself in trouble. The buyers of American Motor cars did not have to purchase another car for so long that the dealerships did not have enough repeat buyers to continue in business. Eventually, American Motors was merged into Chrysler Corporation.

Planned obsolescence has become a part of American business planning. So long as obsolescence is determined by the buyer, this is no problem. If a car owner can continue to run his car and find parts, the use of planned obsolescence causes no difficulty. When planned obsolescence is forced on a consumer, it becomes a burden on society. Currently, effective computer programs can run well for many years. By failing to support certain programs, computer manufacturers have attempted to force replacement. To update the accumulated data and programs when a new system is required need such an unnecessary cost in time and cost that many applications must start over. The added expense will cause some to quit producing.

It is vital to understand that economies are current economies and do not allow comparisons between different times.

CHAPTER FIFTEEN

More About Money

A REDEFINITION

By THIS TIME, you will have realized that this organic point of view differs significantly from the point of view that economics is a study of the distribution of scarce goods. That difference involves a change of definition. That new definition is economics is the study of human activity. The human activity referred to must have an objective that can be accomplished with the use of an economic item—and that no item has any economic value unless it produces such activity.

This different point of view requires a change in the roles of some of the other definitions that figure so significantly in economics. Money is described in conventional economics as a medium of exchange, and the exchange is the basic unit of the study. Money requires a different definition in organic economics. That definition can be said to be that money is the benchmark of value both within an economic structure and between such a structure and the larger organism of which it is a part.

In an earlier chapter, we quoted a book concerning the effects of soldier's money on the economy of Mindanao at the end of World War II. It showed the effects to be devastating when the value of the currency could no longer serve as a reference point for value. Maintaining the value of money in ways that people can relate to it is essential to maintaining a sound economy.

Specie is another word for cash or coin or other money. Such money, in whatever form, must be easily used to transact a business deal immediately, without reference to any other thing or activity. In colonial Virginia, there was little specie in the form of English pounds. For quick and easy transactions, they used tobacco. New England used the Spanish real, or piece of eight, so called because it was designed to be broken into eight pieces or "bits"—whence we get two bits, meaning a quarter—if the need arose for smaller denominations. Under the mercantile system then in force, trade with any foreign country was illegal. The possession of Spanish money inferred that there had been some trade with Spanish dependencies and that they had broken the law. In that case, the people of New England could not pay the stamp tax without admitting that they were criminals.

In Virginia, on the other hand, the specie was tobacco or claims upon tobacco. Tobacco had a value that was regular and could be exchanged for other things at any time by transporting it to England. Tobacco was divisible. Exchanges could be made for one leaf or a whole platform. Tobacco was stable; it could be stored and kept for long periods of time. All these attributes made tobacco a medium of exchange and a handy form of specie.

But tobacco had an additional attribute that enhanced its value. A person could relate his assets and his income to the value of tobacco. Since his total income included so much tobacco, he could decide how much more he needed or how much he had to reduce his outgo to keep within his income. The value he assigned to the tobacco he owned corresponded to the value of the amount of the tobacco owned by every other person in the community. Tobacco allowed the integration of each part of the economic system of Virginia with the whole.

This role of money is different from the common idea of a medium of exchange. It is the idea of a stable reference point for value. It indicates a different role for money in the integration of an economic system.

At this point, we can determine the cause of the American Revolution, not as blamed on taxation of Americans by British, but as blamed on the manner in which the Americans were assigned the impossible task of paying taxes without money to pay them. That impossibility was not known to the Parliament that imposed the stamp tax. For the New Englanders to pay the tax, it would mean they would be subject to imprisonment. For the Virginians to pay the tax, they would have to send tobacco to England, exchange that tobacco for coins, ship the coins back to Virginia, and then pay the tax. The tax receipts would then be shipped back to England. Had the Parliament had any member who was familiar with the situation in

America, they could have been made aware of the situation and avoided the irritants that made the Americans rebel. No taxation presentation, then, was not a battle cry, but a plea for understanding. That the plea was not heard meant that Parliament lost its influence in America.

GRESHAM'S LAW

The role of money as a reference point for the apportionment of resources within the economic entity and between different entities is a role of coordination. As such, it cannot share its role with any other entity. Coordinating roles require that one and only one source of activity be allowed to exist. The price of tobacco in England often varied as other needs were raised by the English. To use both English coinage and tobacco as the backing for money meant that the price of documents could never be determined in advance. A colonist who needed to record a document could never be sure how much tobacco he should take with him to a closing to acquire the coinage that would be required to pay for the record.

Since coinage would never have a constant value in terms of tobacco, it was impossible to value it over time, so the more constant value of the tobacco caused the colonists to eliminate coinage and hold on to tobacco. Later, economists noted this phenomenon and restated it as "bad money drives out good." This law is called Gresham's law.

PAPER MONEY

If a Virginian bought a piece of land from a seller for two hogsheads of tobacco, it is possible that he really didn't need to physically move the hogsheads from his own farm to the seller's. That movement was not really necessary and involved a great deal of effort. As long as the two farmers trusted each other, some evidence of ownership of the tobacco was all that was needed. A warehouse receipt would serve for the proof of ownership, and the seller could instruct the buyer later as to what he wanted done with his tobacco. This warehouse receipt became money.

Later, when America went on the gold standard, a gold certificate, like a warehouse receipt, substituted for the actual gold, and our modern system of bills, including silver and gold certificates, became our currency.

THE MINIMUM WAGE AS THE
BACKING FOR THE DOLLAR

In 1932, America went off the gold standard. True, gold was pegged at $35 an ounce, but Americans were forbidden to own gold. Without a benchmark to determine the apparent value of money, money lost its value. The depression was a direct result of the opinion of the people that money could not be relied on to retain any value. Until World War II, there was no way to determine what the value of money was. When America needed the labor of all the people, labor became valuable.

Commodity labor, defined by the minimum wage, allowed people to compare their available labor to a fixed amount of money and determine the value of goods and services available to them in terms that they could understand. At that time, in the eyes of the people, a dollar became equal to the value of something available to them that they could understand. Since that time, money has effectively been backed by the labor of the people. Again, the best and clearest example of the relationship between the minimum wage and price levels occurred during Richard Nixon's presidency, when a change in the minimum wage from $1 to $1.60 caused all prices to advance by 60 percent between March and August.

REPLACEMENT OF LOST MONEY

Money goes from hand to hand—and quite often during that process, it gets dropped. Money is lost in public places, between the cracks in furniture, through bad investments, ventures that fail, bankruptcies, and other waste. Money is invested in prospects that end up having no value. When this happens, the part of the economic cycle that loses the money becomes less able to be part of the overall economy.

Social Security is one way this problem is overcome. We'll look at it in a minute.

First, let's start with business. The Hoover vacuum cleaner has been manufactured in North Canton, Ohio, for many years. When a new plant was needed, they chose to place it in Juarez, Mexico. With such a long history in North Canton and so much invested there, there must have been a reason not to place their new plant elsewhere.

There was.

Every expense that would have to be paid in El Paso—including costs or materials, delivery, etc.—would be the same as that in Juarez except one: mandatory deductions for Social Security for employees who would work Stateside.

This brings me to this conclusion: *Did you know that Social Security is destroying American business?* Yet at the same time, *Social Security is the one program that has made the economy strong for the last fifty years!*

American retirees can remain customers of American business when they become unable to continue to work. Many tourist destinations depend heavily on the retirees who bolster their economy when other work is unavailable in the area. Areas around our national parks often cater to retirees because no one else has both the money and time to visit the parks.

Social Security helps replace lost money without disrupting the economy. The elderly who are no longer able to provide the value that younger people can would be unable to exist without some financial aid that continues to include them in the economy and makes them active participants in it. The value of the money they receive is maintained by tying it to the labor that currently is provided by others, and the value of the dollar is maintained.

Welfare is another means by which funds are provided to those who cannot overcome the inability to obtain money. A mother's contribution to continuation of society demands that motherhood be supported. A husband is expected to fulfill that role, but all too often, the mother feels her responsibilities as a mother are not shareable, the husband is dead, she has married an irresponsible man, or she simply doesn't know what is involved in being a wife. When these things apply, she is not supported by any one of many options or persons, even though her role is crucial. Welfare is an attempt to save the situation.

Such waste is a necessary part of any society. If there is no venture capital wasted on starting up new enterprises, the economy will cease to exist. Whenever there is no conscious goal to raise children, the time and effort required for reproduction becomes a serious problem. Usually there is a conscious effort to support the mother and child, but sometimes children are conceived before the parents are aware of the additional costs in time and effort that is needed. The unexpected results of misusing the privileges of sex end up in unsupported mothers and children. Usually the parents are young themselves and aren't aware of the difficulties they are incurring when they think they are simply enjoying life. As a result, children are brought into the world by a parent or parents who cannot provide for them. The children are put at a grave risk that must be countered. The purpose of some welfare expenditure is to overcome this problem after the situation arises.

Another purpose of welfare is to provide for those who, through no fault of their own, are no longer able to participate actively in the ongoing continuation of the economy. An actual case involves a state representative who had an employee who worked for him for thirty years without paying into Social Security. The employee had no other resources and would have been fired if he complained. At age seventy, the employee tried to retire. Without Social Security benefits, the choice this employer gave him was to continue work or nothing. He tried to continue working, but couldn't. This would have been the purpose of welfare, but the employee starved before it could be instituted.

The value that is developed by a money system must be made available to those who would otherwise be unable to participate, or the system, like a bleeding body, will die.

Another need for adjustment in the system arises in a different way. A worker picks apples in October, but he must eat in February. If he is to pick apples the following October, there must be a way for him to buy food in February. When we have money that we need later, we bank it until that need arises. When General Motors reduces production because of slow sales, it banks the skill and training of the employees it does not temporarily need by unemployment insurance or vacation. Prior to the Depression, each time the auto companies reduced labor needs, employees were placed on their own resources. No company could absorb the costs of insuring the return of their employees because the additional costs of insurance would make the competing auto companies more profitable and reduce the company's ability to continue operating. The federal requirement that all companies contribute to such a fund, without exception, made it possible for these companies to retain the skills and training that would otherwise be lost. The loss of these skills and training would have acted as a bleeding sore in the economic organism.

Let's return to the earlier premise. This is the essence of an economic scissors. One blade is the fact that no individual will willingly pay any more money for a good or service if he can pay less for the same quality and type of purchase. This rule sets a maximum return for an investment. The other blade represents the rule that if someone else has lower expense, he can sell the product for less. And as you will remember, if a plant in Juarez, Mexico, can produce a product for only its normal costs and a plant in El Paso, Texas, using the same labor, materials, and overhead must pay Social Security, there will be no plant in Texas.

If a plant in a major market using minimum wage labor can produce a product and sell it locally, no plant away from the market, and also using minimum wage labor, can compete if it must also pay transportation to the market. This scissors action creates urbanization and destroys rural economies. While American urbanization had advanced, at one point, to where five counties in the United States supported 20 percent of the population, that concentration has been mitigated by the Social Security system that returns some of the earnings from urban areas to the rural economy.

It is different in Mexico. In Mexico, there is no rural economy (there, money does not exist, and resources have been used up), and even the urban areas contain many situations where no investment is possible. Illegal immigration from Mexico into the United States is a direct result of this effect.

CASH FLOW

The maintenance of an effective cash flow throughout the whole economy is essential to the continued existence of that economy.

An effective cash flow is a part of the "after transaction" economy. "After transaction" can be said to be price. This is to be distinguished from the "before transaction" economy. "Before transaction" can be said to be value. Understanding the difference between the two economies, before and after transaction, is essential to understanding the effect that each has upon the other.

Once a transaction has occurred, an entirely different set of rules and requirements is in control than what occurs in the economy before the transaction. After-transaction economics is controlled by prices that are already determined. That determination is based upon considerations that are part of the before-transaction economics. Before that point, values must be reported in ranges of price. A buyer will pay up to a certain price. A seller will sell down to a certain price. The value of the transaction will be in a range of values between the price a seller will accept and a price that the buyer will pay. This means that identical goods will sell at different prices to different people. As you will remember, if I am offered a pencil at $10 dollars, and I need a pencil badly, I may pay $10 for it. The seller may have only one pencil left after I buy mine, and only one person is interested in it. If he will only pay ten cents, the seller may sell that identical pencil for that amount. Both sales are within the value range of the before-transaction economy. The after-transaction economy has a different value for one pencil than the other. That price is now set in stone.

Once the price is set in stone, there are some different considerations to be concerned with. Every transaction involves a source of the funds and their disposition. This movement of the funds develops a flow that requires physics rules to understand rather than static studies. For example, physics shows that cars traveling at sixty miles per hour take half as much roadway to handle the same number of automobiles as a roadway where traffic is limited to thirty miles per hour. A dollar that is used in a transaction on each day of the week is counted seven times as often as the same dollar used only once per week. The first supports seven dollars in goods and services, while the second supports only one. There is only one dollar in specie in either case. The study of "post transaction" economics, then, includes an understanding of not only the quantity of specie available, but also the frequency of its use.

There is another aspect of post-transaction economics. Every transaction has both a source (credit) and a disposition (debit) of funds. For this reason, all the expertise developed in conventional accounting comes into play. Included in this expertise is the nature of expenses as opposed to assets. This aspect leads to the study of economic waste. Waste is essential to the continuation of the economy. Every setup and teardown expense is a waste, yet without these expenses, no economic progress could exist. Normal wear and tear of specie and mistakes of bankers also reduce the quantity of money available for the continuation of economic activity. Bankruptcies, casualty losses, and deterioration are normal aspects of economic activity. The quantity of specie available for use in activities is constantly being reduced.

In the past, this problem was addressed by finding and mining gold or other resources to convert into specie. The history of America during the turn of the twentieth century revolved around the efforts to make specie of the metal silver. "Cheap money" states, principally those who mined silver, tried to have silver as a backing for the dollar as well as gold. Politicians recognized Gresham's law, where good money drives out bad and stopped this effort, but the problem of accessible backing for money continued.

During the 1920s, frantic economic activity created the illusion that this problem was solved, but the slowing of that activity in the 1930s created a period of Depression. Subsequently, the requirement that people work without the right to spend their earnings during the Second World War created a reserve of funds that fueled a major expansion during the next decade. As these funds became exhausted, a new credit system of store accounts allowed the expansion to continue. As this became exhausted, bank lending continued the phenomenon. Credit cards eventually increased the availability of specie again. The current lack of available funds to the next generation makes it clear that there is still a problem.

The class economy of the elderly is at a much higher dollar level than the level of those who have recently finished high school. Of those things that both groups need, such as housing, the ability of the younger group to compete is sharply limited by the ability of the older to pay and support much higher prices. This forces the younger generation, at least those without familial support, out of the housing economy.

This problem has been addressed in the past by various means. Social Security removes funds from the normal activity of the economy and uses it to cover certain types of waste. Welfare and unemployment insurance cover more. The insurance industry provides a means of covering certain types of waste. Government projects such as NASA inject specie into the system. All these efforts provide a counter to the continuous loss that an economy suffers from waste.

Post-transaction economics has another attribute. Since every fund exchange has both a source and disposition of the money involved, statements of economic activity that do not balance are, by nature, incomplete. The complete report, such as an annual report, will appear to be precise and carry a feeling of certainty with it. Confusion between the seeming certainty of mathematics and the reasonableness of statistics allows this appearance, but it is false. There is nothing certain in statistics or in how the numbers are reported and recorded.

THE THIRD DIGRESSION AGAIN

At this point, it is necessary to return to the second digression and restate a few important points. Post-transaction activities are measured by statistics. People often confuse measurement by mathematics with measurement by statistics, and this confusion creates a real problem.

The introduction of set theory to arithmetic created a difficulty for teachers of mathematics that has not been overcome to this day. Mathematics is a language that requires certain basic assumptions. Among those assumptions is that mathematics is certain and precise. To be precise, a corollary must exist that says that each unit in mathematics is discrete and separate from every other unit and that every unit is identical to every other unit. This precision allows relationships to develop that are certain and sure. The nature of the integer (the unit) allows the learning of those basic relationships in math.

Percentage math also allows a certainty, but percentage math is more difficult to understand than plain math because it no longer has a basis in the integrity of the integer or unit. Each amount used in percentage math is based on a different unit, though it is still called 100 percent. A percentage of one unit may be exactly the same as the percentage of another unit, but because the natures of the units are different, the amounts that result must be different. Henderson County, next door, had 38 percent. Buncombe's actual gain was Buncombe County, North Carolina, had a growth rate of 10 percent with 17,000 people, while Henderson's was 16,000, because Buncombe started with 170,000, and Henderson started with 48,000. Since the units were different, the results were different. This distinction is vital in understanding the nature of economic structures.

But statistics is not math, and neither is it based on any certainty. Use of the same words in math and statistics gives the illusion of comparability. The actual circumstance is that they are based on entirely different concepts. Statistics is not based on the unit, but upon the empirically discovered rules of the laws of large numbers. These laws revolve around the fact that after observing a certain number of objects (or units), numbers tend to repeat themselves rather than having new numbers show up. This is what I mean: Since almost all people are between four feet and eight feet tall, and there are only forty-eight inches between those extremes, it is only logical that after forty-eight people are measured, there will be at least two with the same height. The laws of large numbers are based upon the fact that among forty-eight people, there are not likely to be twelve people over seven feet and twelve under five feet, so the numbers in the middle will repeat far sooner than any others. This means that measurement by statistics has no certainty. What it has is an ability to compare the likelihood of what it measures to be inferred.

AND NOW, BACK TO THE SUBJECT: A REVIEW

These statistics are by nature incomplete. To get as complete a picture of the economy as possible, the numbers must arise from many sources and dispositions, yet many transactions will be left out of that picture.

Post-transaction economics is based upon the transaction; pre-transaction economics is based upon the economic structure. Economic structures have the attributes of organisms.

Each organism has common characteristics that belong to all. All organisms exist in a particular environment. Each is made up of many specialized parts, which may be organisms as well. Each requires nourishment and a means of disposing of what is no longer useful to it. Each retains a structure that is stable and defined. Each renews itself by disposing of parts not working and building replacements. Each leaves a seed, spore, or other reproductive body that enables replacement when the organism no longer can function. The nature of an organism enables a person to identify it as an organism and differentiate it from any nonorganic material. The characteristics of an organism require that all the items mentioned above need to be present.

An economy exists in a particular environment. All economies have many parts, which may be economies as well. An economy flourishes if there are resources to nourish it, and it produces waste, which must be disposed of. Economies are stable with definable limits. An economy recruits new businesses to replace failures. Books and experts define the activities of economies, and entrepreneurs allow replacements. The nature of an economy can enable people to recognize it as an economy and differentiate it from other economies. All the requirements that apply to an organism are present in economies. To study economies as if they were organisms is appropriate and to be desired.

The histories of many countries bear this out. China has a long history in which there is a continuous alternation between the concentration that develops from monopolies in a stable situation and the chaos and revolution that occur because of the need for relief from such concentration. Mexico and other Spanish-American countries have the same pattern of stability and chaos. England had its War of the Roses and stability under the Tudors, followed by the English Civil War. Where stability prevailed for long periods, an inflexible social system developed that restricted everyone to specific roles. Such a system arose in Japan. Prior to the opening of the country to the west in 1854, the country was divided into regions ruled by and synonymous with their lords, the daimyos, each of which developed a place for every citizen. If the citizen chose not to fit into that role, he was subject to death.

The economic organism develops with certain unchanging rules. All activities are determined by the perception of value. Value is a determination of need and exists as a yes/no decision. That decision can be stated as, "Do I value greater than that?" What I give up has to be less valuable to me than what I receive. This decision consists of two parts: first, do I have the value that I can give up to consider this transaction, and second, what relationship does this value have to the overall value available to me? Here, money gives us a reference point. At no point will an economy allow anyone in it to spend more than he has or can get. This rule, that if your outgo exceeds your income, your upkeep will be your downfall, is an inflexible and controlling rule of economics.

Money, then, has a real and important role to play in economics that is not limited to being a medium of exchange.

CHAPTER SIXTEEN

Zen versus the Apocalypse

PROJECT PLANNING AND PERPETUAL MOTION

WHEN ANYONE BUYS a gallon or tank of gas at a service station, the full tank of gasoline can be divided into individual molecules. To do that would be impossible for us in practice, but it is very revealing when we think of it that way. Each molecule burns at a different time, and its economic value is based upon that burning point, when it actually fulfills its objective, making the car move. When it burns, the molecular explosion pushes the piston and causes the engine to turn. This is the reason to purchase gasoline in the first place.

Each molecule has its own history. One was extracted as part of a crude oil barrel in Kuwait, another from crude oil in Mexico or Texas. Other molecules of the same barrel were separated and went into street pavement or became part of a polyester thread in a shirt. After a long process, that particular molecule, along with others just like it, arrived at your service station and entered your car. Until you burned it, as you drove, the value was always a potential value. At the moment it burned, it showed its value. Once it burned, it lost its value.

Like a railway carrying goods, the refineries and oil wells involved in producing that molecule of gasoline exist to move the gasoline and other products of crude oil from their source to their final uses. Production at these facilities is continuous. If there is no specific attempt, we would never identity a specific part of this flow. The process does not allow us to look at any particular molecule of the oil as separate from any other one. The idea of continuous flow is similar to the Buddhist idea that all nature continues to flow, and we are a part of it. A good word for this idea is zen.

The opposite idea of continuous flow is that everything is coming to a climax. We find this idea exemplified with a house. When we build a custom house, we do not expect that there will be another house just like it. There is a start, a set of actions, and a finish. Once the house is built, we do not expect to see the process continue. Even though the builder may build many houses, each is separate and stands alone. Every such project comes to an end. An actor, when the show closes, often suffers depression from the sudden change in his life. This idea of a separate project that comes to an end is exemplified in religious references to the apocalypse, where each thing comes to a final point.

Process activity (zen) and project activity (apocalypse) are two entirely different ways of looking at the world. To many people, no matter how vital, process activity is boring. We read books based on murders because a murder can be identified and a solution of a specific, identifiable situation is dramatic. We look for closure and attempt to bring the world to a tidy, understandable, controllable size. Once we do this, however, we start the process all over again. When we have read the murder mystery and solved the plot, we buy another book. While we like to think of life in this dramatic fashion, we have to live it in continuous but unromantic fashion.

One of the problems of project activity is success. Polio was a crippling disease during the time of World War II. The March of Dimes looked for money to combat the disease. When vaccines were found that eliminated the problem, the March of Dimes was left without a focus. Instead of disbanding, it chose to focus on another problem: birth defects. It is only human nature to want things to continue, but when the objective is accomplished, we have to make adjustments.

There is a distinct difference in the outlook of the two ways of looking at the world. People who look at the world in zen fashion typically do not find themselves at a loss when death occurs. Because they feel that death is a part of life, they are able to continue functioning without feeling that they have been deprived of something important. People who look at life from the apocalyptic point of view, however, require grief counseling and other aids to overcome their fear of loss.

Project activity is necessary when events threaten our lives. When we discussed the Civil War, we found that it was the threat to their continued economic life that caused the Midwestern states to so vigorously pursue it. The dramatic and climatic role of slavery in that war we found to be an illusion. However, the publicity and inclination of people to believe that the war was fought on higher principles than "money" gave slavery the role of villain. Slavery was not abolished, but only changed in form—from slave to sharecropper. That was overlooked. As an apocalyptic nation, we always need see ourselves as accomplishing a noble purpose.

Sometimes the purpose appears silly. Over $1,000,000 was spent once to free three bowhead whales from the ice in Alaska. Publicity had made them a cause célèbre, and the news media followed the case day by day. The project was successful, and the whales were set free from the ice. They swam out to sea, and the press proclaimed the success of the operation. Then Eskimos, who had been in real need of whales to butcher in order to survive the winter, immediately chased, harpooned, and killed them—but the efforts had "saved the whales."

At other times, apocalyptic thinking has had devastating results. The disaster of Prohibition in the early part of the twentieth century created a profitable business out of the destructive use of alcohol. Americans decided that alcoholic beverages had to be destroyed and passed a law to that effect. The law was followed only by those who firmly believed that laws have the effect of solving a problem. For those who believed otherwise, breaking the law became a game that was fun to play. Respect for the law was destroyed, and crime became fashionable.

Efforts to clean the pollution from power plant smokestacks have produced acid rain. It works this way. When coal is burned to produce electricity, acid and alkali are separated. Without intervention, as they cool, they reunite into salts that precipitate as soot. The resulting salts are unsightly, but they can be cleaned up and do not cause any irreparable harm. Scientists have found ways to remove particulates, which are alkaline, from the smokestacks. When only the alkalis are removed, however, the substance that remains is acidic. The result is "acid rain." Acids must find alkalis to become stable again, but there are no alkaline substances available to use. Life cannot exist in a totally acid world, and our efforts to change the world have resulted in destroying the very thing we claim is what we want. This is one illustration of how efforts to make the world conform to human ideals can be disastrous.

OVERCOMING THE REALITIES OF THE WORLD

We believe that we can solve problems. This is an arrogant idea, but human nature tends to feel that the ability to influence and manage life means that we have the power to do so and the right to do what we want. This idealization of the power of humans to overcome the realities of the world they live in arises from two sources. The first is the need to establish coordination of human activities.

Since it is important that one person not destroy the efforts of another, coordination is essential to survival of the species. Humans have such diverse interests and ways of surviving in the world that we often feel the need for dramatic episodes to obtain cooperation in such a diverse group.

Coordination can be attained by establishing common objectives. Politicians often use this method to make their country conform to their ideas of what is important. To fight terrorists is such a method, even though it is a negative one. No positive result can occur when everyone is concentrating their efforts in avoiding problems that have and will be part of our lives as long as human beings exist. Although only a few are actually involved in the duty of fighting terror, everyone is expected to make it top priority at the expense of every other objective. This does not accomplish what is needed, but does distract people toward what the politician wants.

The second idealization is a misinterpretation of what we call scriptures. Scriptures are those myths, legends, writings, and common ideals that illustrate the expectations that people have about one another. These ideals are essential to human coexistence, but cannot cover every situation, nor can they be applied to every circumstance. Interpretation of these moral norms—whether from the Bible, Koran, Torah, Bhagavad-Gita, or any other statement of expectations—allows the misinterpretation that it is all inclusive. This in turn allows the user to feel that there is only one way to act. Moreover, by determining the interpretation of the scripture to mean whatever the user chooses, there is a weapon available to cause people to support the arrogance of that user.

One of the oddities of this situation is the emphasis of the Bible, when taken as a whole, to condemn the villainies exemplified in that part of the Bible (Chronicles through Esther) that shows how people should not act. However, people find these villainies attractive and almost invariably choose to follow the example of the villains rather than recognize that these actions make real coordination impossible.

Use of scripture to require unattainable goals is a frequent problem. This story explains how: A certain woman had a happy marriage, a healthy daughter, and a good life. She was pregnant for the second time and enjoying a camping trip, when she suddenly became very ill and lapsed into a coma. After a quick trip to the hospital, the doctor found that she would not recover from the coma as long as she remained pregnant. They performed an abortion, and the woman recovered. Allergy tests determined that she was allergic to hormones produced during pregnancy, and she was warned never to have another child. This woman did what is considered now a despicable thing—but survived.

The idea that any law that was ever written can cover all situations is very human but also very arrogant. Current efforts to prohibit abortions would have penalized the doctor in that state for his action. In saving the woman's life, he would have been subject to fines and jail time because the procedure he used to save her life was illegal. Some people would prefer to exert their world view on life and death and would second-guess the doctor. They would have prevented the doctor from saving the pregnant woman because what he did was what they believed was "wrong." They would prefer to reduce the availability of medical help for those who need it by penalizing specific actions that are necessary at certain times, and not entirely depend upon the judgment of the doctor, who has been trained to recognize a life-or-death situation. This reduction of resources is an economic event directly resulting from the idea that morality and laws can cover all possible circumstances.

THE ROLES OF GOVERNMENT AND RELIGION

Confusion over the roles of government and religion illustrates the difficulty in determining what is best for humans and how to achieve it. One of best supports of the economy of the United States is the idea of the separation of church and state. Certain catch phrases, such as "The government governs the best when it governs least," tend to indicate that the role of government must be limited. By involving itself in a nonessential area such as abortion, a government law would limit the positive effects of medical expertise without any offsetting value. Given this effect, we need to look closely at the objective of having a government. What is it that the government is required to do?

The objectives of government are threefold. The first is to eliminate threats to the survival of society. Police and legal systems are directed toward this. The second is to do the things that are necessary collectively when they cannot be done individually. The third is to provide a mechanism to allow resolution of differences in order to allow coordination of actions. None of these objectives demands action when a situation does not affect society as a whole. When moralists demand a law to cover something that, in their mind, is a threat to society, they direct government into areas where it cannot be successful. As long as society can survive without the law, the law will either restrict life or be ignored.

The alternative is uncertainty. When the zen point of view is involved, uncertainty occurs when there is a change that affects the value of the product. During the time that a process is producing something that is valuable, all the certainty that is required for economic activity is on hand. The sudden arrival of uncertainty causes people to look for certainty in other places. When the product that they relied on, and its related processes, lose their value—as with buggy whips and steel production—people have to make some adjustment and look for certainty elsewhere. Usually the places where they expect certainty are in religion and government.

Certainty cannot exist. Project (apocalyptic) thinkers understand this. Real estate salesmen know that every prospect will not result in a sale. If one sale in fifteen tries is successful, they may consider themselves successful. The ability to live successfully with uncertainty is a hallmark of the entrepreneur and essential to all people at some time in their lives. It is also the basis of feeling confident that life does not have to be lived in fear.

We have talked about how certainty is an essential part of every life. On the other hand, the services of people with a process attitude, and a need for certainty, are essential to the continued success of our society. Homebound mothers, teachers, policemen, factory workers, and others need to know that they will receive a sufficient amount to live on so that they can continue to contribute to their world. These people do not need to be wealthy, and needs are not the criteria for ensuring that they have sufficient resources to contribute. The nature and quality of what they contribute is the controlling factor, not their needs.

Socialism includes the phrase "To each according to their needs." The appropriate phrase should read "To each according to their willingness and ability to contribute." A clear example of where this difference would be evident is in the matter of college scholarships. Financial ability has no relevance when expectations of a student are based upon what his contributions are likely to be to society. Here, getting financial support for attending college should be dependent on a prospectus of the student's intentions, not his needs. That the prospectus can change should be accepted. The important point is that they intend to contribute to their society.

College is not for everyone. In fact, some studies on higher education in India indicate that economies cannot absorb more than 7 percent of the population in academic endeavors. The use of college monies for individuals who have not determined that they will contribute to society in the future is an unacceptable waste. The expectation that they know how they will contribute is unnecessary.

LABOR AS A COMMODITY

When the discussion was about the nature of a gas molecule at the beginning of this chapter, the gas involved was called a commodity. Some things are not commodities. One-of-a-kind artworks cannot be replaced with a substitute. The ability for something to be replaced easily is required before something can be called a commodity.

Agricultural products or natural resources like oil, corn, other grains, and any item that does not require that a specific item be specified is given this designation. To be a commodity, it is only necessary that there be no differentiation between one item and all other items like it. A baker needs flour for his product, but if one bag of flour isn't good, he simply purchases another. This definition of commodity not only fits these products, but most labor as well. An individual can be a carpenter, bricklayer, clerk, or any other worker, including doctor and lawyer. His labor will be used, but is not unique to him. Others can do the same job, and he can do other jobs. This type of labor is a commodity.

Commodity prices are subject to large changes if quantities are increased or decreased. Apple prices are fixed by the need people have for apples, the price people must pay to obtain the apples, or the possibility of obtaining those apples for less money. An apple orchard owner in North Carolina had a full warehouse of apples and decided to empty his warehouse by selling the apples at a ridiculous price so that buyers would move them quickly. While $16 a bushel is needed to cover all the costs of production, and $6 of that cost is spent in picking the apples, the orchard owner offered his apples to buyers for $4 a bushel. There was a quick sale from his warehouse, but buyers were then unwilling to pay more than $4 for any other producer's apples as well. An orchard owner would have to spend $6 to have the apples picked and receive only $4 after they were delivered. Apples rotted under the tree because no sensible grower would spend $10 of his own money just to do business. He couldn't.

Solutions to the problem of oversupply vary greatly. When milk prices become too low, farmers have been known to pour their milk on the ground to avoid further lowering of prices. Many producers have invested in advertising to increase usage of their product, but workers don't have that option. They have formed unions to stabilize the price that they receive for their labor. Labor unions have been a boon to the economy because they have stabilized wages to the point that workers could remain on the job and be a part of the economy.

FARM INTEREST

A further example of what happens when zen and apocalyptic thinking interact can be found in agricultural financing. Farm income is apocalyptic; farm interest is periodic. Each year on the farm is a separate project, with a definite beginning, growing season, and harvest to complete the cycle. Production loans and crop insurance together allow the financing of the yearly crop to be closely allied to the production of the farm, and at the end of the season, these financial factors can be settled up.

Capital improvements on a farm that last beyond the crop year do not act in this way and are the most serious risks that farmers take.

Farmers must buy land, build barns, and buy equipment that cannot be covered by the successful production of a single year. When this happens, the relationship between the project income of the farmer and the periodic requirements of the banker is influenced by the mathematical scissors. When crop receipts are high in one year, there is no difficulty in matching the income of the farmer with the interest due to the bank. However, when the income of the farmer drops significantly in the second year, the requirement of periodic interest becomes destructive. What is logical in the first year can mean bankruptcy in the second.

This mechanism was described in the first chapter of this book in an account of the situation in Gaul at the time of the fall of the Western

Roman Empire. The same mechanism also occurred at the time of the dust bowl during the Depression. Mortgage foreclosures on farms forced farmers to leave Oklahoma and other affected states and created the migratory "Okies," who eventually settled in California. To balance the income of the farmer to the interest and payments due to the bank in lean years is essential if we are to have a stable economic situation in farming.

We, as part of an overall economy, need to determine the objective of that economy in allowing farmers to farm and recognize that their contribution to the economy deserves the adjustments needed to keep them going.

CHAPTER SEVENTEEN

The Nature of Vestment

INVESTMENT, DIVESTMENT, VESTED INTEREST

A PROFESSOR TAUGHT PRINCIPLES of economics. A student noticed that although the supply side of economics was covered well and amply, the demand side of economics was not covered at all. After noticing this, he asked the professor about the possibility that the demand side of economics be given equal play. Had a study about the nature of the demand side been done? The vehement response of the teacher was that the economist had to stop somewhere, that we could not study the whole of economics as fully as we would like. This puzzled the student as the professor was a competent teacher.

In an inspired moment, the student realized the motive behind that response: the professor might have needed to review all that he had learned as well as learn new and different economic principles if the idea was pursued energetically. Had he been required to take the time to adequately study this different point of view, he would have had to invest much more time without receiving any income. He would have had to restudy the subject and reorganize it into a new course of study.

The professor spent many years developing the lesson plans that made it possible to stand before students and explain what he learned. He expected that this investment would provide an income that would continue over a period of time. Like everyone else, the professor's living was an economic structure. He had so much income and so much outgo. It is important to remember that his outgo could never exceed his income.

Economic structures deal with resources and needs. Of these two, the most necessary is income. The student's question indicated that there was more to be studied, and the idea of a new and different interpretation of economics was a direct threat to the investment he already made in his studies and profession.

His concern about relearning economics was based on the need to retain the resources upon which he lived. This involved spending time and study without income. The professor would have had to go without income for a period of time before he could teach what he newly learned or relearned what he had been teaching. His economic structure was based upon the information he had already accepted about economics. The income he received and used to pay his bills came from his previously established understanding and ability to teach economics. That he would not want to lose what he had invested is not surprising.

Although each student in each class was a new and different challenge, the professor's lesson plans were developed to cover all the possible questions and insights that a student in the class should assimilate. Each student had his own course to follow in life, and each was different from all the others, but the investment the professor made would cover a particular time and study that would fit into that person's life. By continuing to enroll students in his classes, the professor could expect to continue the same course of study for many years. Each time he repeated the course, he could expect to receive income that would cover his outgo.

Investment, vested interests, and divestment are words that relate to the process or goods will fulfill and continue to fulfill the objective of an investor over a period of time. An investment is expected to provide a resource to accomplish some objective of the investor. Investment of a husband or wife in a marriage relates to the objective each wants to fulfill. If those objectives coincide and support each other, there will be a good marriage. However, if a husband wants to maintain an active life, continuing to work and be among people, while his wife wants to live in a solitary world away from people and wants him there with her, either one or the other will be frustrated. In this case, the investment will not return its value.

The vesting concept is most easily understood when the investment is in stocks, bonds, businesses, or other financial goods and processes. (Direct investment in services cannot occur. That investment would be in the knowledge of process that provides the service.) Investment can occur with any objective, however, as we have illustrated above. Investment, without a clear definition of the objective of the investment, can be frustrated. That clear definition must coincide with reality as well.

REALITY—PERCEIVED AND ACTUAL

Several times we have referred to the element of reality. We have mentioned that it is the perceived reality that matters in economics, even if it differs from the actual reality. In investments, this is true as well. We invest in children, in homes, in relationships, in knowledge, in processes, and even in stocks and bonds. We make our investments based upon what we perceive to be accurate, and that accuracy is based on our past experience, tempered with advice, information, and concepts we accept as true. Because we have accepted these background ideas as true, we fight for them, whether they are actually true or not. What mother, after investing her life in raising a child, will easily accept that her child is a crook and should be in jail?

Bad investments are often based on bad information. An individual who decides to rehabilitate a house may expect to pay $20,000 to accomplish that goal. When he is required to invest $60,000 instead, he has the choice of trying to recover his cost or accepting the realistic understanding that people will not pay that much. By accepting the actual reality, he can sell at the lower price and move on. In many cases, however, he will choose to ask for the higher price and have an asset that no one can use.

PART FOUR

INVESTMENTS WE NEED TO MAKE AS A COUNTRY

CHAPTER EIGHTEEN

What Do We Need to Do?

THE STRENGTH OF OUR COUNTRY IS
THE STRENGTH OF OUR PEOPLE

BEFORE THIS POINT, we were principally interested in the theories involved and in the bricks that make our country great—the individual economy. We have stated that each person is an economic structure and that each structure is a part of the overall economy. Practical applications of the point of view have been only been touched on. In such a case, why should we be concerned with these theories? The answer to that question is they have very practical applications, and here we start to discuss them.

This book is incomplete. To be complete, every economic structure, every complication of demand, and every cultural factor in economic activity would have to be analyzed and explained. Like history, a full analysis would take more time to write than the events that are being recorded. Like history also, there must be a point of view that allows the significant ideas to be explained so that they can be acted upon.

The point of view of this book is that sound individual economic structures make sound economies. Since economic structures must have more resources than needs to exist, the assurance of threshold amounts of resources for all individuals is the secret of a sound economy. Threshold amounts are the amounts of resources that make it possible for a person, family, or business to continue to exist. They are not affluence. Affluence is, and should be, a result of contributing to the economy over and above what is required.

The result of this different point of view is recognition of flaws in our economic system. Individuals who must pay for inventory and then pay taxes on the money that has been spent for inventory will not willingly invest in inventory and find themselves in debt. People who can avoid paying Social Security by moving their business across the Rio Grande will not continue to invest in domestic production. Prisoners in penal institutions who benefit from their incarceration will not willingly change their attitudes, and by being imprisoned actually benefit from causing problems for society.

Some means that people use to acquire their threshold amounts appear to be sinful to other people. A convict who has murdered and is in jail, where he has no reason to want for food or shelter for the rest of his life, has established an economic structure. His resources are assured, and his demands are met. Society has chosen to allow him to benefit from his crime. Unless it is to a person's advantage to act responsibly, he will never contribute to his economy, except as a parasite. These means of assuring the threshold amounts should be made unprofitable and others substituted.

Resources and needs are not necessarily financial. The prisoner above has an assurance that his needs will be met. That assurance is a resource. The investment a mother makes in a child may require that she support that child, even when the child becomes offensive to others. Without the possibility of reinvesting in another child, the child has become her only resource. Time spent mowing a lawn is an economic transaction, even though the resource involved is time, and that is exchanged for the need of a mowed lawn. No measurable activity has occurred, but economic action has taken place.

There are a series of remedial actions that need to be taken to assure the soundness of the American economy.

PRISON REFORM

Prisons can be built for a number of purposes. We can punish those who have hurt us, we can eliminate competition, we can enforce our beliefs on those who differ from us, we can be sadists and attempt to hurt others, and legitimately, we can attempt to prevent future threats to society by separating those who would harm it from the rest of us. Several of these reasons are counterproductive.

Punishing those who have hurt us is a waste of resources, since what is done is done and cannot be undone. By providing means for one drug lord to eliminate another by turning him in is counterproductive. Beliefs are not subject to change by force. No one should be allowed to harm another, especially with official support. The only remaining purpose is to protect society from future harm. Activities in the realm of prison usage, then, should be consistent with that purpose. A recent blurb in the "Dumb Crook News" describes a man who walked away from a minimum-security prison with only a day left on his sentence. Instead of the "Dumb Crook News," this should have been recorded in the "Dumb Prison News." This man was facing an uncertain future without any expectation of receiving what he needed to survive. By walking away and thereby assuring himself of getting an additional sentence, he is secure and free from any concern about his future for several years.

If a man believed that sex was a punishment leveled against women, a majority of women would consider him deluded. So it is with people who believe that providing necessities for those whom you must lock away to safeguard society is punishment. They think that such "punishment" will deter prospective prisoners from activities that will provide food in profusion and all the shelter they need. No matter what the background, if the prospect of enough food and all that they consider necessary is offered to an individual who has no other possible means of acquiring resources, that individual will choose the sure security of the circumstance that they can become used to, in this case, prison.

For such people, incarceration must be more realistic. No matter what situation people find themselves in, there is a threshold of resources that they need to exist. But any greater amount of resources should always depend on the contribution the individual makes to society. Such a minimum in a prison is adequate food and a place to sleep. If any prisoner wants more, even exercise, the additional demand should be subject to additional contribution from the prisoner.

Such contributions should start with cleaning and maintaining his own cell and cooperating with the authorities. They could then proceed to more advantageous contributions, which could include working on projects that could compete with other workers.

The idea that work that provides incentive and worth to a prisoner creates unfair competition—because prisoners are paid less wages and are given what they need—seems to make people resist accepting it. Every contribution to society, however, frees someone else to contribute more. This understanding allows a different point of view of the idea that prisoners working while in prison would benefit society. There are many occupations that are unique to prison life, but the lack of a wide range of trades available to them should not prohibit finding work for prisoners. By requiring contributions for all privileges above the threshold amount, prison would be far less attractive to those who otherwise would look to it as a way of life.

SOCIAL SECURITY

Let me start with a note to the reader: As the author of this book, one of my credentials is that I have been a CPA for over thirty years. During this time, I have audited or participated in businesses in twenty-two states and have lived in eight. I've looked beyond the rules of accounting, tax, social security, and economics as they are presented, and I am an expert in the areas that are mentioned below.

Back to our subject: As you remember, we said that Social Security is destroying American business. *Yet at the same time, Social Security is the one program that has made the economy strong for the last fifty years!*

Furthermore, Social Security is the factor that has stabilized American society for fifty years or more. Individuals with a reduced ability to work are not eliminated from the economy, and their capacity to be active customers assures a stable supply of profits to businesses. Social Security has some flaws, however, as all successful programs do.

The first remedial action for Social Security is to require that imports into the United States pay the same taxes and abide by the same restrictions as domestic businesses. The current situation in this country, as in many other countries, is that protectionism is reversed. At this time there is no such thing as free trade. Where previously we charged tariffs to protect American business from foreign competition, now we charge taxes on domestic production that prevent competition with foreign business.

Where countries importing to the United States have equivalent taxes for similar purposes and restrict their businesses in the same way as the United States does, unrestricted trade might exist, but a simpler method would be to apply the tariffs in the same way and to the same purpose as domestic businesses. Exports would be given credit for such taxes.

The current situation with Social Security, required benefits, and other tax requirements for domestic production is analogous to the situation in Spain immediately after the defeat of the Amada. Spaniards paid taxes on anything they manufactured, while the English were able to import into Spain and avoid these same taxes. The Spanish economy could not and never has completely recovered.

If you follow the product cycle from initial action to usefulness, you will find that, for Social Security purposes, every part of it, except rents and royalties, is considered earned income to someone, and the amount to be taxed would seem to be the total value for customs purposes. For America to avoid a result similar to Spain's, tax expenses need to be equalized. This can never be exactly equal, but the tax for Social Security applied to the invoice amount of the import would be an overcharge for that tax and an undercharge for other requirements, such as employment security and workmen's compensation expense. The net effect would be closer to equality.

This simple rule would avoid another scam that is costing Americans many additional income tax dollars. Here's one way to amend the situation described in a hypothetical case: Juan and Jose are brothers. Juan manufactures a product in Mexico for a dollar. If he had sold it directly into the United States, his price would have been $4, and he would be taxed on $3. However, he sells it in Mexico to Jose for $5. Jose now imports it into the United States, using the price on Juan's invoice, and sells it for $4. Under our NAFTA free trade rules, there is no tariff or import tax. By doing this sham transaction, Juan and Jose can split the real profit, $3, and do not have to pay either Social Security or income tax. Social Security is not required in Mexico, and there is a loss in the United States.

There is an additional advantage politically to including imports into the base for Social Security. The increased source for funds to pay Social Security benefits means that there is less required from each participant. In turn, Social Security taxes can be reduced. As every reduction in Social Security rates increases the take-home pay of domestic as well as imported production, the effect of a Social Security tax cut will be felt by every taxpayer immediately.

CHANGES TO THE INCOME TAX

Capital Gains

The next series of remedial actions relates to the income tax. Willie Sutton robbed banks. When asked why, he said, "Because that was where the money was." Although taxes are intended to help fund things that people need, the same principle should apply to income taxes. Current tax thinking is based on the accounting principles that are easily available rather than effective accounting principles that reflect the ability of the taxpayer to pay. Generally accepted accounting principles are used for good management, but are not applicable to taxes. As an example, depreciation is intended to determine whether a major move by a business, such as the purchase of a car, results from sound thinking (the purchase lasts longer than was planned) or poor planning (the purchase must be replaced before it was supposed to be). Neither of these results has anything to do with whether there is money to pay taxes or not. Tax levies should be designed to rely on sound tax accounting principles and not on management accounting.

An actual experience where this difference created a problem for the taxpayer occurred several years ago, when a landowner decided that he would harvest one acre of forest land each year and replant it. The operation required a truck and chain saws, which cost $3,000. Management accounting required that the equipment not be deducted until it had been used because it was required to be matched to the income that would derive from it. In any one year, the income from the sale of wood from one acre of land as the landowner intended to use it would be $2,000. After the first year, the owner would have spent $3,000 for equipment and received only $2,000 for his efforts. However, the tax laws would say that he had only used one-fifth of the value of the purchase since trucks last five years. He would have had a tax income of $1,400 ($2,000 minus $600). He would owe a tax at 15 percent of $210 and a Social Security payment nearly equal to the same amount, a total of around $400 on money that was spent and was no longer available to be used for taxes.

Since he had no money to begin with, he had to look at other options for his land. He found that if he sold the timber, as a block for a clear cut, he would receive $12,000 for the sale. Capital gains laws eliminated the Social Security tax, and his tax at 15 percent was only $1,800, which left over $10,000 available for him to use. Thus, tax laws have been a major cause of clear-cut timbering.

Investment Relief

As in the case above, investments in plants and equipment require funds when they are purchased. This is before any money is received from their use. A deduction to allow a deferral of this expenditure, when funds are received, would be in order. Nonetheless, if anyone could easily purchase equipment equal to the amount that they would otherwise have to pay tax on, they could avoid all taxation. Because of this, the idea of allowing a complete deduction in advance for invested funds would be unwise. However, government, whatever else it is, is a partnership between each of the people as individuals and all the people represented by the elected officials. It would seem that an allowance for half of the net taxable amount would alleviate the problem exemplified by this example. This would allow deduction of the cost of investment currently.

When the investment is sold, tax would be due on all money received except that which has not yet been deducted. The purpose of capital gains is to avoid paying tax on the "profit" from inflation. Since all deductions and receipts would be in current dollars, the need for capital gains provisions would be eliminated.

OTHER TAX CONSIDERATIONS

In order to accomplish a really fair income tax system, tax laws need to be changed. There are five major basic changes in the tax laws that would make it easier for people to engage in businesses. These consist of depreciation and investment relief (discussed above), inventory relief, dividend relief, timing changes, and common tax rate schedules. Let's take them one at a time:

Inventory Relief Changes

Inventories must be purchased to begin most businesses. The requirement of using management accounting in the valuation of inventory creates a situation where the individual, in order to begin business, must first spend the money needed for inventory and then spend the same money for tax on what has not been sold. It may be news to some bureaucrats that money can only be spent once.

To alleviate this problem, an adjustment for inventory items should be added to the calculation. If an inventory changes from one year to the next, the changes should be an additional deduction if the inventory is increased and an additional income item if the inventory has decreased. Such an adjustment would defer tax on money that has already been spent and include all deferred income in the year in which it disappears from the inventory.

This approach differs from cash accounting methods by ensuring that fraud is not covered by the manipulation of inventory.

Dividend Relief Changes

At one point, wages provided 85 percent of the basis of the federal income tax. The remaining 15 percent was made up of dividends, rent, royalties, interest, and all other sources of income. Despite this comparative unimportance, well over one half of the text in the tax code is related to the matter of dividends. There is a good reason for this. Dividends are not income, and it takes a lot of verbal manipulation to make them taxable under income tax laws.

When a father goes to work and provides the income for a wife and children, he transfers that income from his efforts to people who spend the money. If dividends are income, every transfer of funds from the breadwinner to any other member of the family should involve a taxable event. A corporation is designed to be a breadwinner for its stockholders. When it transfers the income to those who have a claim on it, it is not and cannot be legitimately considered income.

Over half of the income tax code could be eliminated if dividends were deductible by the corporation, and individuals received dividends tax-free. Alternatively, corporations could be denied the deduction, but dividends would be taxed to the recipient. Moreover, the number of foreign corporations who place themselves in other countries to avoid tax on their transfer of income would decline.

Timing Changes

April 15 is a dead-letter day (that is a red letter day and a deadline) with every taxpayer. Information for wage earners that has already been sent to the IRS must now be sent again to provide a second form for people to fill out and the IRS to keep track of. CPAs and other accountants must work day and night for three months in order to fill out the forms, even though the IRS already has the money. This drastic uniformity cannot be correlated to the actual conditions of the business or of the wages involved.

An individual who has been given a W-2 that shows the amount of earnings and taxes paid knows that the IRS has a copy of the form and should not be required to file the same information a second time. If the amounts on the W-2 are appropriate for the income and exemptions of the individual, why should he pay good money to have the same information sent on a return? Obviously, if a W-2 was filed one year and not the next, the IRS should check with the wage earner to see if the employer failed to file, but the tax should not require extra work on the part of the taxpayer.

A change in the deadline would be helpful as well. Taxes should be due and payable on January first and past due on December 31. Payments not made by the due date would have the highest interest rate available for each complete month thereafter. A small penalty should be assessed to encourage early filing when filing is necessary.

Common Tax Rate Schedules

A man with a small child will use a "Head of Household" schedule to calculate his taxes. A married couple must use a ""Married" schedule, and singles must use the "Single" schedule. By living as married (without the legality) and filing single schedule returns, families can manipulate their taxes and pay less than those who abide by the laws. The situation arose because certain states required that income from married couples were considered as earned equally by both. All taxpayers need to be treated equally, and the privilege was expanded to all states without any analysis of the nature of the change.

The concept behind community property in the states where it is law is that the partner who is not working contributes to the success of the earning partner by supporting him or her in those things that would have reduced the earner's income. Limiting the concept to only married people was the result of a misconception that only married people acted this way. One individual provides the effort to earn resources, and the other takes care of the first by providing food and other services that would detract from the first's ability to accomplish his goals.

When we look at this analysis, we see that attaching this rule to any legality, such as marriage, fails to fulfill the purpose of the rule. The purpose can only be met if the individuals involved are allowed to file jointly if the situation exists. If there is no state law that limits certain people to using the rule, any two people should be allowed to file jointly. The head-of-household schedule would be allowed to file jointly so that that schedule would not be needed, and the right to choose single or joint returns to all people would be based on one schedule.

Other substantial changes to the tax code might be helpful, but these are needed.

SALES TAX DIFFICULTIES

Other tax problems involve sales taxes of states. Currently, the only requirement to avoid sales tax on purchases in any state is to purchase the item either by mail from another state or over the Internet. Local retail establishments cannot compete when they are required to pay the same prices for their merchandise as the online supplier and sales tax as well.

Unfortunately, the interstate commerce clause in the constitution does not provide for states to tax outside their jurisdiction. Such taxation must come from the federal government, which has prohibited states from applying their tax laws to such sales. States that rely on the sales tax have found that they are unable to provide education and health benefits when there is not enough money to pay all the bills.

Internet suppliers have rightly asked not to be required to abide by these taxes since each jurisdiction has the opportunity to tax at a different rate, and local sales tax rates are so varied. Local jurisdictions may have the right to add to state sales taxes, and there is no possibility of following all the laws.

In such a case, a relatively equitable solution would be for the federal government to tax all Internet and out-of-state sales at a set rate, such as 4 percent (4%), and distribute this tax to the destination state. Such a solution would be simple to administer and allow the states to provide the services that the state is required to provide.

HOW TO DEAL WITH MONOPOLIES

Cancer in the body occurs when one part of the body can eventually acquire all the resources needed by every other part. Earlier chapters described the nature of the problem, but essentially, as with an organic disorder, it is important to keep a proper balance so that all parts of the whole—as in this case, the economy—can continue to function. We do not need to assure this balance by a duplication of functions, but we do need to assure that all resources do not come locked up in one business and become a monopoly.

There is no possible reason for people to pay excessive prices for monopolistic products. The monopoly is as stable as the government, and we have a benchmark in government financing. When governments borrow money, it must pay a certain interest rate. Monopolies have no reason to earn more than the government and should be limited to that yield on their sales. A monopoly should be limited to earnings—including payments to officers who can decide what will be spent—of no more than the yield of government bonds if the goods or services provided by the monopoly are essential to the health of the economy. If government bonds and monopolies have similar characteristics and risks, there is no reason that the investments in each should not be equivalent.

THE MINIMUM WAGE

By now you understand that the minimum wage is essential as a backing for our money. Twice I have illustrated that it is the only commodity that has a fixed value in money, that it is the reference point for determining the comparative value of all goods and services within the economic structure, as well as the comparative value between economic structures.

Unfortunately, as with all cures for ills, organic or economic, there are side effects. When the two barbers, Mr. A and Mr. B, have the same revenue, Mr. A has a far higher profit than Mr. B. After Mr. B has paid his rent, he must use the remaining money to pay all his expenses. Mr. A also owns his home and a restaurant, so his expenses are almost nonexistent, while Mr. B must compete with Mr. A for all that he has to buy. Any addition expense that is required, such as transportation, has the same effect.

This leads us to the issue of urbanization. Because of the mathematical scissors, additional costs always give an advantage to the economic structure without them. Let's review. In the case of the minimum wage, the costs for labor throughout a country are the same in every location. When the costs of transportation to the market are added to this, the economic entity that is not located in the market is always at a disadvantage. As time goes by, the distant enterprises continue to fail, and the effective enterprises become more and more concentrated in the urban areas. As a result, since the end of World War II, when the minimum wage became an effective backing for the dollar, migration to the cities has resulted in five counties or cities in the United States having 20 percent of the population of the United States.

As long as the minimum wage continues to be an effective backing for the dollar, as it should be, there must be some method to allow for alleviation of the side effects. One possible method would be to allow a reasonable reduction in the minimum wage for entities that are a reasonable distance from defined markets. An example would be that a 10 percent reduction of the minimum wage is allowed to enterprises located fifty or more miles from a city with a population of fifty thousand or more. Since this is also an effective commuting distance, it should allow businesses and people to relocate away from the concentrated area.

There is also the problem of assisting handicapped people to contribute to society. If the same wage must be paid to all workers—as the minimum wage requires—there are individuals who are outside of this criterion. Some of these people may be unable to accomplish the employer's needs, and the employer can have difficulty finding the money to pay for their services. If the employer cannot find the money to pay an employee, he will either terminate his employment or go broke. While he may not be able to pay for the work that an individual can do at minimum wage, he may be able to continue to employ him at a lower wage. The minimum wage should be flexible enough to allow this. Alternatively, other sources of funds for employing handicapped worker that do not rely on productivity must be found.

The same situation applies when an employee is new on a job. On-the-job training requires a period when productivity is not enough to pay the employee the full minimum wage. The Job Partnership Training Act was designed to meet this difficulty, but employers misused the funds involved to terminate trained employees and hired unskilled ones in businesses where training was easy. This mining of the plan could have been avoided if the minimum wage was flexible enough to allow employers to pay a lesser wage to new and untrained hirees. By manipulating the system, some employers were able to pocket half of the new hiree's wages.

One additional problem with the minimum wage is its interaction with welfare and unemployment benefits. If a laundry was able to pay minimum wage for people to man the laundry, and the available welfare benefits were larger than the minimum wage, there was no incentive to work. Talkeetna, Alaska, has a shortage of motel workers during the summer season because welfare is sufficient for most of the available employees. Here, the proper solution would be to increase the welfare payments for winter months and eliminate them during the tourist season. Although the total cost of the benefits involved would remain the same, the lack of payments during the time that employees are needed would encourage productive employment.

DRUG ENFORCEMENT

When Will Rogers commented that Baptists and bootleggers would vote dry as long as they could stagger to the polls, everyone thought he made a good joke. But good jokes have to have a basis in reality. This reality was that both Baptists and bootleggers benefited from laws prohibiting the sale of alcohol. Baptists benefited by having a clear symbol that they were cooperating with each other and that they were successful in "resisting evil." Bootleggers benefited by eliminating competition and increasing the price of their product. (Here we must remember our first digression and overlook the morality of the issue.) The fact that any action is stupid, immoral, or illegal does not mean that it does not exist. Bootleggers could include in their resources the laws that increased the resources available to them.

Food, tobacco, alcohol, and drugs share a common characteristic. Demand for them is constant. All must be acquired on a regular basis. Food is a natural requirement, but the other three attain their demand by becoming addictive. This addiction can be avoided by not starting to use them, but once addicted, the user finds he cannot avoid obtaining the substance without the severe penalty of withdrawal. This penalty is far more compelling than any law.

The economic structure of the pusher is secure as long as his resources cannot be touched. One means of touching those resources is to interdict the supply of drugs, but this is inefficient. There is seldom enough information to accomplish this. No user is going to reveal his source since there is no likelihood of avoiding the penalty of withdrawal if his source of supply is interrupted.

We have no sure way of finding out what is actually happening if those who know will not talk. Moreover, the strength of the economic structure of the pusher is such that law enforcement is more often susceptible to joining the pusher and becoming an integral part of the problem than would be believed. Often, it has been alleged that the law enforcement departments are divided so that while one part is fighting drugs, the other is pushing them. We can only avoid the appearance of this reality if we attack the economic structure of the pusher. We cannot succeed in eliminating the problem if we only appear to be fighting the problem itself.

The first strength of the pusher's economic structure is the assurance that no user will turn him in. As noted, the penalty for doing this is a real and physical sickness called withdrawal, if not retaliation by the pusher or someone in his organization. This is common enough in NYC, et al. Currently, there is no offsetting benefit to the user. Even the idea that he will receive a reward is unsure and far away. The fear of withdrawal is immediate and frightening. Until this problem is dealt with, access to cooperation from users, who alone are in a position to know what the situation is, cannot be expected.

The idea that drugs are "evil" is a hindrance in this case. Whether drugs are evil or good is not relevant to the situation. The fact is that drugs exist and that drugs cause this situation. By accepting the reality of the situations, we can be ready to deal with the problem in a more realistic manner. If the penalty of the user is withdrawal (and withdrawal is a real and vicious punishment), that penalty must be dealt with. An addict must be allowed to continue his addiction until it can be eliminated without penalty. Until this step is taken, any attempt to eliminate drugs will lack the resources of cooperation and knowledge that are essential to do so.

The strength of the economic structure of the pusher is the high prices commanded by the product and the security of the user. Once we have dealt with the security of the user by assuring him of a supply, the next step will need to be the reduction in the price of the product. If the supply of the product is made available to the user at twenty-five cents per dose and the sale of any product at a price above fifty cents is made a crime, the immense fortunes that fuel the activities of the drug dealers will evaporate. The price of the product must be made into a negative resource rather than the source of immense profit. I have mentioned this before, but it is important enough to repeat.

A third step would be to reward the individual who assists in dealing with a pusher. A user does not necessarily turn in a dealer who has, as it seems to him, been making what he considers a necessity available to him. Unless he shares in the confiscated amounts of drugs, he has no real incentive to assist in removing the problem.

The waste of prison space for drug dealers is a drain on the taxes paid by every honest taxpayer. Prisons should not be used to house and feed people who can easily pay for their own needs. A far more appropriate punishment would be confiscation of their resources. If a pusher is arrested, the proper punishment should be to place all the assets of the pusher in the hands of a trustee who would provide for the legitimate needs of the pusher from his estate. Then all the assets that had been accumulated from drug activity would be confiscated by the courts, but not before a trial would determine the proper amounts. The remaining assets would be returned to the defendant.

These approaches to the problems of drug addiction and drug dealing would be effective.

EDUCATION

Education is an economic activity that is very difficult to fund. It is essentially an allocation of venture capital and a part of the start-up expenses of each person's life. As such, it shares the risk factors of all venture capital. To sell a venture capital enterprise to a competent investor, the salesman has to show what is expected from the investment, what return can be expected, how realistic the expectation that the venture will succeed is, and most important, what the purpose of the investment is. Never will you find an investor willing to part with his money because the principal "needs'" the money. Yet education, typically, does not evaluate the objectives nor base the funding on the expectations from that education.

The first of these expectations is the economic problem of objective. Many educational entities have not defined the result they expect from their educational system. Objectives that appear irrelevant are often determined to be the purpose of the schools. Usually when these objectives are analyzed, they are relevant. Some of the objectives are complete successes when it comes to their primary objectives. Such an objective is establishing a relationship between members of a community. Establishing such a relationship is both an essential role of the schools and a usually accomplished objective. This objective is often overlooked, however, because it is usually not identified.

Other unspecified objectives include the encouragement of voluntary disciplinary efforts such as team playing in football and other sports. To a major extent, this has become a lesson in attempting to make money, but in most schools, the team members are choosing to learn the necessity of cooperation. They learn the necessary discipline with no expectation of reward. To a major extent, this objective is successful.

One of the most overlooked aspects of funding education is the relevance of what is being taught. Pupils attend primary and high schools for twelve years, attend college for four, and maybe become teachers, without once being a part of the world outside academia. For preschool and some elementary grades, this is as it should be, but a math teacher who has never bounced a check is not likely to understand and convey the importance of bank reconciliation. Schools are not producing productive citizens when they fail to understand what is required in being a productive citizen.

Education must be considered as if it were applied venture capital. Students should be required to identify a course of action by which they can succeed in life. By requiring proposals from them about this, they can develop an understanding of need for commitment toward contributing to the society of which they are a part. Schools also can orient their teaching toward assisting the students to succeed rather than blindly teaching what is prescribed by academicians who are only be able to deal with students en masse. This does not require a firm commitment to any particular future course of action, but an attitude of contribution to the society. This is in contrast to an attitude that there is a right to higher education.

REPRESENTATIONAL CHANGES

Earlier, we dealt with the idea that people who do not live in a community are unable to make informed decisions about it. English members of Parliament had no idea that Massachusetts's businessmen could not pay taxes with English pounds when they had only Spanish coins that were considered illegal. They were equally ignorant of the role of tobacco as a currency in Virginia. The cry "No taxation without representation" signified this problem. America has taken great steps forward in developing a solution to this problem, but there are still steps that need to be taken.

Every community is a living, changing group of many people. This means that problems, concerns, and interests change constantly. When people who represent a community are at work far from the community for years at a time, their ability to understand what their constituents want becomes blurred, and some things that were wanted when they started are actually disliked later.

When Tip O'Neill was asked at his retirement whether he would return to his friends in Boston, he was quoted as saying, "I have no friends in Boston." Even if this is an apocryphal story, it illustrates the tendency of congressmen to be unfamiliar with the needs of their constituents. One solution that allows our representatives to be current with the situation where they live is to not allow congressmen to run for an office while they are in office and require them to physically live in the district from which they are elected a certain number of days before elections—in effect, an eligibility issue making it possible or impossible for them to run for congressman.

Living in their home district would be advantageous for voters even if it was necessary to double the representatives' salaries and allow that increase to be deferred for the term they are not eligible to run. If two eligible individuals alternated terms, then the understanding of the community that elected them and the experience that they would develop would be both maintained and enhanced.

The second place where representation needs to be improved is in Electoral College voting. Currently, a candidate for president can be elected by a slim majority in only ten states. The sense of the constitution implies that each district would give its vote to the candidate who wins in that district. Because each district has its own needs, the Electoral College is our assurance that no one district or group of districts could eliminate the voice of other districts in enacting laws. Such a change would enhance this concept and allow better coordination on the national level.

Argentina and England are among the countries where government is centralized in certain cities. Buenos Aires has such control over the lives of Argentineans so that only those who live in that city can have an effective say in the government. London has recently allowed Scots and Welch people to have a limited say in their own countries. It is interesting to note that both these areas have become attractive to new population moves. The need for responsive government is not a factor in only one country.

WORLD ORDER

The most important interaction between countries is trade. Hindering trade reduces our ability to make the best use of our resources. To make free trade practicable, there must be common understandings about the rules, regulations, and practices that must be followed when commerce exists between any two people. When this commerce involves trade between people of differing cultures, there needs to be a mechanism that resolves their differences. Luckily, there are many people engaged in developing and supporting this concept.

Trade between countries has its problems and side effects, however. While the United States can benefit from eliminating reverse protectionism by charging its taxes on both domestic and foreign production, the countries that use the euro have a different problem. If social programs in Sweden or Germany differ from programs in Spain or Italy, the difference will increase costs in one country and create favorable conditions in another. Eliminating these preferences would require that the social programs in all these countries would need to be standardized. Such standardization usually requires that either all these countries adopt similar social programs or that the European Union be assigned the responsibility for all social programs. Such adjustment will require a great deal of effort.

CONCLUSION

THIS BOOK IS written to ask for serious consideration of these changes. The purpose of each change in the system is not to deride of belittle any other ideas that might be appropriate, but to establish them as starting points to improving our country and our world. Every person is an economic unit. We need to encourage individual responsibility for the health of that unit and provide systems that allow that unit to strengthen itself and every combination, from marriage to a world economy.

It has dealt with subjects that have evolved from a different point of view, but the reader will bring to the ideas in it his past points of view that may not support the investments suggested. The book has tried to explain an understanding of what actually happens in the real world, and it will be up to the reader to accept reality or continue with perceptions that do not square with what is really happening. Use your own experience, set aside your preconceptions, and judge the investments suggested with an open mind.

FROM AND ABOUT THE AUTHOR

Y ou need an introduction to the author.

This book has many insights that could not have come from books, and you may believe that I don't know what I'm talking about when I discuss the nature of monopoly or any other of the concepts that appear in it. So to start,

> As a disinterested outsider, Doyle,
> what do you think of the human race?

When my high school pal asked me this question, I was insulted. Many years later, however, I realize that he had come close to the attitude that has permeated my life. I love people, but as they are—not as they would like to believe they are. The difference has led to many difficulties with people. Some have set standards that they cannot meet and do not want to believe that they have failed insofar as meeting those standards. Others have tried to establish how great they are and fail to understand that past actions indicate that they should not believe their own "PR."

I also have my severe handicap. When I see and react to a problem that others do not see, they tend to be both fearful and dubious about my abilities—as to their existence and usefulness.

I have tried, in this book, to record the understanding of the human race that this handicap and attitude have given me.

I've had a unique opportunity to sample many different ways that people find to work together for the good of their communities. I have also too often been in the position of being dissatisfied with the current economic and political situation and made moves to change them. Unfortunately (and also fortunately), I did not address the problem. I addressed the symptom. As a result, I have experience in farming, construction, retail, government service, personnel administration, hospital finance and operation, teaching, mining, motel keeping, realty, and a number of other fields. As a CPA, I have been involved in auditing major companies in twenty-two states and tax returns for indigents—a very wide range of economic conditions. No person I have ever met has seen as much of the American economic world as it works hands on.

Many years ago, working as a school bus driver, I learned that there are minimum requirements, which, if met, will bring peace and harmony among diverse and difficult people. One of the rules I offer for students is "One does not hit anyone else, for any reason, at any time." The other is "Every person needs to be treated as the person he is, no matter how young he is, or what he believes." The first eliminates fights; the second provides a reason for people to cooperate with you.

My first brush with economics came as a junior in college. After taking the principles course, I asked my professor why the books didn't look at the nature of the demand cycle. Her response—that an economist "has to stop somewhere" and that "your problem is…"—alerted me to the fact that there was an emotional component to her answer. I wondered why, and then realized that her life was invested in the limited theories she taught. I wrote about this experience in the chapter on vesting deals and how an expenditure of time and effort establishes her resources in her economic structure. Thus, my question was a distinct threat to her.

This alerted me to the economic component of all activity. My subsequent exposure to the varied experiences already mentioned were colored, and understood, by my interest in economics. Currently, that has meant a forty-two-year economic analysis of many varied fields of endeavor.

Later, I enrolled in the doctoral program in economics at the University of Tennessee. The same attitude that my principles teacher exhibited existed in others here too. Academic economics is, as it should be, an introduction to a pragmatic discipline that allows the economic community to deal collectively with the practical aspects of the monetary system. This in itself is an economic method of interlocking and cooperating with the world as it is. The value of conventional economics is not to be slighted or ignored.

In my studies, I concluded that the academic economist is right to overlook the ramifications of demand economics. However, the business economist must include the needs for advertising and means of changing demands. This requires him to go beyond the ideas of the academic economist.

My first brush with history occurred at the age of fourteen years old when I won the local award for excellence in history. Five years later, as a junior in high school, I effectively ran the history course for a teacher who was assigned the subject—without any experience. Later I minored in history and obtained a master of arts in education degree with a specialization in history. I later entered the doctoral program in economics at the University of Tennessee. When it was clear that my interest did not coincide with that program, I dropped out.

At a later time, I entered the doctoral program in history at the University of Akron. My interest in history clearly shows up in this book, and my training in the subject is the source of my use of historical background herein.

I also hold a master of arts in education from Western Carolina University and a bachelor of science in business administration, with majors in history, accounting, and general business from the University of Arizona.

My history specialization included studies in Russian, Mexican, Brazilian, and Spanish history. Additionally, I have read on the history of Turkish, Indian, Chinese, Japanese, British Commonwealth and Empire, and many other areas. The economic component of each of these was evident as I read them. When I attempted to work for a doctorate in history, I found that this component was usually overlooked in preference to the dramatic impact of wars and fighting. These preferred studies are the effects of economic circumstances, not the core of the historical activity.

Education has also been a major part of my life. My mother and several of her siblings were teachers, my sister is a retired teacher, a son and a daughter are teachers, and I hold a master's in education. This exposure to education qualifies me to write about the problems that the education system bears.

In religion, too, I have had an unusual background. Raised as the son of a Southern Baptist preacher, I was exposed to biblical analysis sufficient to become member of the church at the age of eight. Having analyzed the Bible over fifty years, I have found that all people are basically trying to be a part of the world they live in. I once served as a deacon in the Baptist church, an elder in the Presbyterian church, a pastor-parish relations committee chairman in the Methodist church, and a vestryman in the Episcopal Church. In addition, I have studied to be a Mormon and a Roman Catholic. The one consistent element in all religions is the attempt to be at peace within the world in which we live.

I have also been active in politics. Since the Republican convention that nominated General Eisenhower, I have failed to be active in party or candidate campaigns only a few times, when I was under the Hatch Act that prohibited political activity by government employees or in service.

At one time, I was given the job of changing over hospital records from a manual system of operations to a computer system. This job was accomplished with only one complaint that took only one programming step to solve. For those who are used to large memories and powerful machines, this would not seem to be an accomplishment; however, this application was done on a machine with only 4800 bytes of memory.

The insights developed from computers can be useful in understanding any system. As my first exposure to computers was in 1966, the application of computers was in its infancy. The development of computer operations had proceeded to the development of the COBOL language.

COBOL is specifically defined, based upon a four-part analysis. The parts are the identification of the system, the environment in which the system works, the processes involved, and the data to be used. Moreover, the system operates in three phases: the development, with its implementation; the operation, when it is used; and the removal, when the hardware is cleared so that a new application can be installed. The insights developed from this circumstance do apply to the economic systems that are discussed in this book.

The background of this book is economics flavored by history, politics, religion, business, accounting, and many other influences written by an individual who has been able to experience these things. I have forty years of experience in the business world. A boss once told me that some people claim to have forty years' experience, when they mean one year's experience forty times. For the economy of the United States to work efficiently, it takes both kinds. There are not enough activities to allow everyone to act as if every year would be different, and many jobs can only be done with the specialized knowledge that comes from having done the job before. Some people who contribute to the welfare of our country have limited knowledge and abilities, yet they contribute what they can. Although I have a different background, I contribute in the ways that I can for the good of my community. This is the responsibility of all people.

There are many other influences to the making of this book. I have had an active role in the following economic activities (among others): accounting (cost, budget, and certified), assembly line work, bookstore sales, consulting, camp counselor, carpenter, corporate controller, computer (design, installation, and implementation) electrician, farm hand and farm accountant (feed lot, horse racing, cotton, pasture cattle, truck and grain), flea market sales, forest manager, nonassembly line factory work, hardware specialty retailing, home builder (successful and unsuccessful), hospital controller (including Medicare), installation of heavy machinery, insurance sales, internal auditor (salt, yam, wire and cable, sound systems, specialty chemicals, leather, drugs) IRS clerk, landlord, motel operations, nurseryman, painter, payroll and personnel administration (private and federal government), realtor, variety store management, soldier (adjutant general's office, supply, reconnaissance, mapping, aerial photography interpretation, tanks, communications, and intelligence), teaching, (college and high school level, principal subjects, accounting, computers, math), temporary employment, and waiting tables.

In terms of research backing my theories, I have included significant studies in accounting, economics, finance, banking, geography, government, history (American, colonial Brazil, modern Brazil, China and Japan, British Commonwealth and empire, India, Mexico, Russia, Spain, and Turkey), investments, math, and psychology.

Because I have such an extensive background, I know I can be accused of bragging. I am reminded of a famous TV line given to Walter Brennan: "No brag—just facts." I've given you the facts, so above all, please enjoy this book.

www.ingramcontent.com/pod-product-compliance
Lightning Source LLC
Chambersburg PA
CBHW071319120626
46546CB00002B/376